The Only Guide to a
WINNING INVESTMENT STRATEGY
You'll Ever Need

The Only Guide to a
WINNING INVESTMENT STRATEGY
You'll Ever Need

Index Funds and Beyond—
The Way Smart Money Invests Today

LARRY E. SWEDROE

T·T

TRUMAN TALLEY BOOKS/DUTTON

NEW YORK

TRUMAN TALLEY BOOKS/DUTTON
Published by the Penguin Group
Penguin Putnam Inc., 375 Hudson Street,
New York, New York 10014, U.S.A.
Penguin Books Ltd, 27 Wrights Lane, London W8 5TZ, England
Penguin Books Australia Ltd, Ringwood, Victoria, Australia
Penguin Books Canada Ltd, 10 Alcorn Avenue,
Toronto, Ontario, Canada M4V 3B2
Penguin Books (N.Z.) Ltd, 182–190 Wairau Road, Auckland 10, New Zealand

Penguin Books Ltd, Registered Offices:
Harmondsworth, Middlesex, England

First published by Truman Talley Books/Dutton,
an imprint of Dutton NAL, a member of Penguin Putnam Inc.

First Printing, May, 1998
10   9   8   7   6   5   4   3   2   1

LIBRARY OF CONGRESS CATALOGING-IN-PUBLICATION DATA:
Swedroe, Larry E.
    The only guide to a winning investment strategy you'll ever need : index funds and beyond—the way smart money invests today / Larry E. Swedroe.
        p.   cm.
    Includes bibliographical references and index.
    ISBN 0-525-94435-4 (alk. paper)
    1. Mutual funds.   I. Title.
HG4530. S894   1998
332.63'27—dc21   97-38908
                                                                          CIP

Printed in the United States of America
Set in Times New Roman
Designed by Eve L. Kirch

*This book is dedicated to
the memories of the greatest man I ever knew,
my father, Jerome David Swedroe,
and my beloved sister Jayne Swedroe.*

Contents

Contents

Part Three. The Winner's Game:
Make Modern Portfolio Theory Work for You

Introduction

On January 20, 1891, the first official game of basketball was played at the International YMCA in Springfield, Massachusetts. Each time a basket was scored, play was stopped while someone climbed a ladder to retrieve the basketball from the bottom of the peach basket. It was not until 1905, fourteen years later, that someone was smart enough to remove the bottom of the peach basket.

For decades individual investors have been trying to beat the market by either actively managing their own portfolios or investing in actively managed mutual funds. The vast majority have done so with about the same disappointing results that the Brooklyn Dodgers had when they faced their arch rivals, the New York Yankees, in the World Series. The rallying cry of the Dodger fans, "Wait until next year," has been adopted by active managers who fail to outperform their benchmarks because "it wasn't a stock picker's kind of year." The problem for both the Dodger fans and active managers is that "next year" has rarely delivered their hearts' desire.

In 1990 the Nobel Prize in economics was awarded to three economists for their contributions to the body of work known as Modern Portfolio Theory. This theory presented every investor with a way to win the investment game without really trying. In fact, Modern Portfolio Theory has demonstrated that efforts to beat the market are not only nonproductive, they are counterproductive because of the expenses and taxes that are generated by the practice of active management. The only winners in the game of active management are the Wall Street firms that generate commissions, the publications that offer "expert" advice, and Uncle Sam, who collects more taxes. Modern Portfolio Theory demonstrated that all investors can have a positive investment experience if they adopt the strategy known as passive asset class investing.

Unfortunately, the media in America have a great effect on the behavior of individuals. While you rarely find in the press or hear over the airwaves a story on the death of a single individual in an automobile accident, every form of media will cover, as a lead, or as a front page story, a plane crash that kills hundreds. This phenomenon may be the main reason so many people are afraid to fly when all the statistics show that it is far safer to fly than to drive. Similarly, the media are often filled with warnings from so-called financial experts that the market is overvalued. These warnings often cause investors to panic and sell, or delay investing available funds, despite the overwhelming evidence that market timing is far more dangerous to your financial health than is a buy and hold strategy. Stocks are only risky if the investment time horizon is short.

It has now been seven years since the awarding of that Nobel Prize in economics, and many investors are still climbing the ladder to retrieve the ball from the peach basket. While many sophisticated institutional investors have adopted passive asset class investing, the vast majority of individual investors are still trying to beat the market through active management strategies. However, as the financial press continues to report on the failure of active management strategies, the tide is starting to turn. As recently as 1994, only 3 percent of individual investor inflows into mutual funds went into index funds. In 1996 that figure grew to 11 percent, or \$24.5 billion.[1] In addition, *Standard & Poor's* (S & P) 500 Index funds are now growing at a rate eighteen times faster than the mutual fund industry as a whole. Investors have obviously noticed that over the past three years index funds that track the S & P 500 outperformed 93 percent of the 2,400 mutual funds that rely on money managers to pick and choose among a broad array of American stocks. Even mutual fund giants like Fidelity and Merrill Lynch, which have long boasted of the stock-picking prowess of their money managers, have moved to offer investors more index funds of their own.[2]

This book provides you with a road map that will hopefully shorten the 14-year journey (the time it took before they removed the bottom of the peach basket) to the winning strategy that is staring investors right in the face. Following this road map will make you a better informed and therefore more effective investor. Part 1 describes how and why individuals invest in active strategies. Part 2 describes the foundation of Modern Portfolio Theory, in other words, how markets work. The remainder of the book is your "Trip-tik" to implementing the winning strategy in a way that will meet both your individual tolerance for risk and your investment time horizon. The choice is yours: you can invest according to theories that have won the Nobel Prize in economics and been deemed a prudent approach by the American Law Institute, or you can continue to climb the ladder to the peach basket by actively managing your portfolio and investing in actively managed mutual funds.

Now that I have described the contents of the book, the following analogy will provide you with an easy way to relate to some of its concepts and help you find the way to the winning strategy.

At a recent tennis clinic I learned something that not only dramatically improved my tennis game, but also provided me with an insight about games in general.

After making what I thought was a great shot, a forehand that landed right in the backhand corner of my opponent, my teaching pro said, "That shot will be your worst enemy." While it was an exceptional shot, he explained, it was not a high-percentage shot for a good "weekend player." Remembering how good that shot felt, I would try to repeat it. Unfortunately, I would be successful on a very infrequent basis. The pro asked me if I wanted to make great shots—or would I rather win matches? (I thought that one was the cause of the other.)

The pro explained that in the game played by weekend warriors such as myself, most points were not determined by successfully hitting the rare, low-percentage shot. Instead, the vast majority of points are lost when balls are hit into the net, long, or beyond the lines, in a failed attempt to hit those exceptional winning shots. That is why this type of strategy produces what is called a loser's game.

In order to improve my results, the teaching pro told me that all I had to do was understand the game I was playing. Since, unlike professional tennis players, I am certainly not capable of consistently hitting winning shots, I was playing a loser's game. Instead of trying to hit winners (and end up hitting the ball long, wide, or into the net), I should just try to hit the ball safely back, with a bit of pace, and utilize the middle of the court. Let the opponent play the loser's game. Recognizing the brilliance of his insight, I immediately put his advice to work, with astonishingly good results. I was now regularly beating players with whom I had previously experienced difficulty.

What does tennis have to do with investing? Simply this: like any game, consistently successful investing requires a successful strategy. The vast majority of individual investors (and unfortunately even most professionals) try to beat the market. They do so by attempting to uncover individual securities they believe the rest of the market has somehow mispriced. They also try to time their investment decisions so that they are buying when the market is "undervalued" and selling when it is "overvalued." Such a strategy is known as active portfolio management. Occasionally, with the same infrequent timing of my great tennis shots, these active portfolio managers will make the proverbial killing. On the other hand, over the long run, they will lose more often than they will win. Just as in loser's tennis, the only way to be a successful investor is not to play the loser's game. If you begin with an open mind, you will conclude that active management is this loser's game. If you decide to play the loser's game, the only people you will be enriching are your broker, the manager of the actively managed mutual fund or portfolio in which you are investing, and the publisher of the newsletter, magazine, or ratings service to which you are subscribing.

In this book you will see that there is an alternative strategy to the loser's game, one that the most sophisticated investors use. This winner's game accounts for over one trillion investment dollars. It is based on over forty years of research by the leading financial economists in the world, which culminated in the awarding of the Nobel Prize in economics in 1990.

This book will provide the skills necessary for you to play the winner's game. Applying this strategy will require three commitments on your part:

- You must be willing to be patient with your portfolio. The financial markets are volatile. The longer the time horizon, however, the more certain you can be that the expected outcome will occur. Equity investments are only risky if the investment time horizon is short.

- You must have confidence in your strategy so that you will have the discipline to stick with the approach throughout the inevitable bad days.

- You will need the courage to ignore what I call the investment pandering put out by Wall Street firms, trade publications, and market gurus.

Much of what you will read in this book directly contradicts conventional wisdom—ideas that have become so ingrained that no one questions them. I am confident, however, that if you keep an open mind you will find the evidence presented here so overwhelming that you will be convinced of its accuracy. Remember, "The earth is flat" was once conventional wisdom. Legends do die hard.

I am also confident that you will acquire all the essential knowledge you need to win the investment game, beat the professional money managers, and sleep well while achieving your financial objectives.

Thanks for coming along, and I hope you enjoy the ride.

PART ONE

♦

THE LOSER'S GAME—

The Game Wall Street Wants You to Play

Anyone who thinks that there's safety in numbers hasn't looked at the stock market pages. —Irene Peter

♦

Like everybody else in this industry I have an ego large enough to believe I'm going to be one of the select few that will outperform. —George Sauter, Vanguard Group

♦

The investment business is, by definition, a business of hope. Everyone hopes that he can beat the market, even if few people actually can. —Avi Nachmany

♦

A fool and his money are soon parted. —Traditional

CHAPTER 1

◆

Why Individual Investors Play the Loser's Game

The most costly of all follies is to believe in the palpably not true. —H. L. Mencken

It is undesirable to believe a proposition when there is no ground whatsoever for supposing it true. —Bertrand Russell

Of all the words of mice and men, the saddest is it might have been. —John Greenleaf Whittier, "Maud Muller"

Galileo was an Italian astronomer who lived in the sixteenth and seventeenth centuries. He spent the last eight years of his life under house arrest, ordered by the church, for committing the "crime" of believing in and teaching the doctrines of Copernicus. Galileo's conflict with the church arose because he was fighting the accepted church doctrine that the earth was the center of the universe. Ptolemy, a Greek astronomer, had proposed this theory in the second century A.D. It went unchallenged until 1540, when Copernicus published his major work, *On the Revolution of Celestial Spheres,* which stated that the earth rotated around the sun rather than the other way around.

History is filled with people clinging to the infallibility of an idea even when there is an overwhelming body of evidence to suggest that the idea has no basis in reality—particularly when a powerful establishment finds it in its interest to resist change. In

9

Galileo's case, the establishment was the church. In the case of the belief in active managers, the establishment is comprised of Wall Street, much of the mutual fund industry, and the publications that cover the financial markets. All of them would make far less money if investors were fully aware of the failure of active management.

Most investors, investment advisors, and portfolio managers engage in active management of their investment portfolios. They try to select individual stocks they believe will outperform the market. They also try to time their investment decisions by increasing their stock investments when they believe the market will rise and decreasing them when they believe the market will fall. These investors, advisors, and portfolio managers attempt to beat the market through active management strategies despite an overwhelming body of academic evidence that has demonstrated that only about 4 percent of returns are due to individual stock selection (finding undervalued companies) and only 2 percent of returns are due to timing the market decisions (shifting assets into and out of the market or between asset classes). A study by Gary P. Brinson, L. Randolph Hood, and Gilbert L. Beebower, "Determinants of Portfolio Returns," demonstrated that fully 94 percent of returns result not from market timing or stock selection but from "asset allocation" decisions (how assets are allocated in a portfolio).[3]

Asset allocation is the process of determining what percentage of your assets are allocated, or dedicated, to what specific asset class. An asset class is a group of assets with similar risk characteristics. Asset classes can be as broad as cash (or its equivalent, such as a money market fund or a treasury bill), bonds, or stocks. Alternatively, they can be more narrowly defined. Bonds can be divided into short-term and long-term. Stocks can be divided into such categories as small companies and large companies. They can also be split into categories such as growth companies or value companies (a term I will fully explore later). They can even be more narrowly defined into such categories as small value and large value companies. Adding the broad category of domestic versus international, one ends up with such categories as U.S. small value and international large value. Investor decisions about the allocation of assets among available asset classes is by far the major determinant of the risk and the returns of a portfolio.

Considering that one academic study after another has demonstrated that about 94 percent of returns are determined by asset allocation decisions, one has to wonder exactly why individual investors, and the majority of professional money managers, spend virtually all of their time trying to pick stocks and time the market. I will shortly examine the causes of this peculiar behavior.

If you had a heart condition and your doctor offered you a choice between two drugs, an old drug with a 6 percent chance of success, or a new drug with a 94 percent chance of success, which would you choose? What would you say if I told you that you can get the 94 percent solution for your investments, and that this solution is the result of over forty years of academic research that culminated in the awarding of the 1990 Nobel Prize in economics? What would you say if I told you that you could increase returns and reduce risk at the same time? Would you be surprised if I told you that the solution did not require a degree in financial economics, and that it was based on a common sense approach that every investor could understand? Given the availability of the 94 percent solution, one is confronted with the enigma that the majority of investors choose the 6 percent solution, active portfolio management. I believe that there are several cultural phenomena contributing to this peculiar behavior.

(1) The Black Hole of Knowledge

Most Americans, having taken a biology course in high school, know more about amoebas than they do about investing. Despite its obvious importance to every individual, our education system almost totally ignores the field of finance and investments. This is true unless you go to an undergraduate business school or pursue an MBA. My daughter is a senior in an excellent high school, and she is graduating very close to the top of her class. Having taken a biology course, she can tell you all you would ever need to know about amoebas. She could not, however, tell you the first thing about how financial markets work.

Just as nature abhors a vacuum, Wall Street rushes in to fill the void. Investors, lacking the protection of knowledge, are susceptible to all the advertising, hype, and sales pressure that the investment establishment is capable of putting out. The problem with this hype is that, in general, the only people that are enriched are part of the investment establishment itself. As you will discover, the vast majority of investment firms and mutual funds (and, I am sure, individual investors) consistently underperform the simple *Standard & Poor's* 500 Index. This index is made up of the stocks of five hundred of the largest U.S. companies (hence the term "S & P 500"). It is often considered a proxy for the market itself. It is, therefore, the most-often-used benchmark against which the performance of active managers is judged.

One well-known Wall Street advisor, Robert Stovall, when asked about Wall Street's underperformance, responded: "It's just not true that you can't beat the market. Every year about one-third of the fund managers do it." He then quickly added, "Of course, each year it is a different group."[4] Amazing! How is the average investor to know which group of fund managers will succeed?

In 1995 almost 85 percent of professionals failed to beat this index, and that's prior to paying the income taxes that their trades generated. Consistent underperformance is one reason why mutual funds have been created to mimic the performance of the S & P 500 Index. For obvious reasons, such funds are called index funds.

(2) Hard Work *Should* Produce Superior Results

A second factor in this behavioral dilemma is the great faith in the Protestant work ethic. To quote my ex-boss, an otherwise intelligent and rational man: "Diligence, hard work, research, and intelligence just have to pay off in superior results. How can no management be better than professional management?" The problem with this thought process is that while these statements are correct generalizations, efforts to beat the market are an exception to the rule. If hard work and diligence always produces superior results, how do you account for the failure of the vast majority of professional money managers (all bright, intelligent, capable, hard-working individuals) to beat the market year in and year out? In the face of all this evidence they continue to give it the old college try. The lesson: never confuse efforts with results. As you will see, hard work is unlikely to produce superior results because the markets are efficient.

(3) Behavioral Economics

When the vast majority of active managers underperform their respective indexes, why do individual investors continue to place over 90 percent of their funds with active managers? Richard

Thaler, an economist at the University of Chicago, an advocate of "behavioral finance," attributed this behavior to *overconfidence.* "If you ask people a question like, how do you rate your ability to get along with people? Ninety percent think they're above average. Ninety percent of all investors also think that they're above average at picking money managers."[5]

Professor Thaler and Robert J. Shiller, an economics professor at Yale, note that "individual investors and money managers persist in their belief that they are endowed with more and better information than others, and that they can profit by picking stocks. While sobering experiences sometimes help those who delude themselves, the tendency to overconfidence is apparently just one of the limitations of the human mind."[6] This insight helps explain why individual investors think they can identify the few active managers who will beat their respective benchmarks.

There are other behavioral reasons why investors choose active managers. Somehow, investors feel that by not selecting an actively managed fund they give up the chance of being above average, and the vast majority think they can at least do better than that. Individuals also like to be able to blame active managers when they underperform, yet be able to take credit for choosing the active managers who happen to outperform the market.

When asked whether fund managers were also overconfident, Thaler responded: "All fund managers think they're above-average money managers. Active fund managers can't believe that markets are efficient. Otherwise they would have no reason for existing."[7]

(4) Playing the Market

Another reason that Americans choose the 6 percent solution, curiously almost in opposition to the work ethic reason, is that they love to gamble. Americans love lotteries, Las Vegas, wagering on sporting events, and so on. That is why you hear the term "play the market." Serious investors never play the market; they invest in the market. Serious investors do not care that a passive (buy and hold the market) strategy is boring. They do not look for the markets to provide them with excitement. Instead, they look for markets to produce returns commensurate with the amount of risk taken. Serious investors follow the advice of Girolamo Cardano, a sixteenth-century physician, mathematician, and quintessential Renaissance man, who said: "The greatest advantage from gambling comes from not playing at all."[8]

(5) The Gambler's Fallacy

Investors also fall prey to what is known as the gambler's fallacy, the idea that winners ride "hot streaks." Of course, there is no proof of that idea, either in gambling or investing. As proof that selecting mutual funds that beat the market is not the winner's game, Mark Hulbert, publisher of the *Hulbert Financial Digest*, a newsletter that tracks the performance of investment newsletters, put together a portfolio of "market beaters." He chose managers who had managed to beat the market in the preceding year. That portfolio earned a 99 percent return over the next 15 years. Not a bad return, except for the fact that a portfolio of "market losers," those funds that lagged the market in the previous year, returned 350 percent over the same period. In contrast to these seemingly impressive returns, the stock market as a whole rose about 600 percent over the same period.[9]

(6) The Cocktail Party Story Syndrome

Finally, many investors choose the 6 percent solution so that they will have a great cocktail party story to tell. Of course, you never hear about investments that did not turn out well.

There is only one way to beat the loser's game of trying to select individual "undervalued" securities or trying to time the market: Choose not to play that game.

CHAPTER 2

◆

Active Portfolio Management Is a Loser's Game

The value of an idea has nothing to do with the sincerity of the person expressing it. —Oscar Wilde

An idea is not responsible for the people who believe in it. —Don Marquis

All great ideas are controversial, or have been at one time. —George Seldes

No matter how thin you slice it, it's still baloney. —Alfred E. Smith

For better or worse, then, the US economy probably has to regard the death of equities as a near-permanent condition. —*Business Week,* August 13, 1979, with the Dow Jones Industrial Average (DJIA) at 875.26

In building their investment portfolios most investors pursue one or more of the following alternative strategies:

- They select individual stocks based on their own research, advice from a broker, or on a "hot tip" from a friend.

- They choose mutual funds based on their past performance, particularly chasing the hot money managers.

17

- They rely on the recommendations of trade publications such as *Forbes*, *Money*, *Smart Money*, *Worth*, and the *Wall Street Journal*.

- They rely on fund ratings by such services as Morningstar, which rates funds using a star system similar to the one used by film critics.

- Finally, they rely on the advice gleaned from newsletters to which they subscribe or "market gurus" who appear on CNBC and elsewhere.

I will explore each of these strategies in this chapter.

Individual Stock Selection

A recent study by economist Terrance Odean suggests that individual investors aren't as bad at stock picking as many people think. They're worse! The study covered almost one hundred thousand trades from 1987 to 1993 and found that the stocks individual investors bought trailed the overall market and the stocks they sold beat the market after the sale. The longer the time span, the more their performance trailed the market. Investors shot themselves in the foot with their trades even before taking into account the transaction fees and taxes they paid for the privilege of "playing the market"—costs that further depressed trading performance. The author's conclusion: Individuals shouldn't be trying to pick stocks. He further stated that investors probably don't realize just how badly they are doing. Since they are trading in a rising market, their portfolios generally showed gains. Unfortunately, the time and money they spent trying to pick stocks cut into their profits instead of enhancing them.[10]

Relying on Past Performance

One obvious approach to predicting future performance is to rely on historical results. Why not just buy the shares of a mutual fund, or a group of funds, that were the top past performers? A study done by SEI Corporation reviewed mutual fund performance for the two successive five-year periods 1981–1985 and 1986–1990. They found that mutual funds that finished in the top quartile of all funds in the first period had about an equal chance of finishing in the *bottom half* of all performers in the succeeding period as they did of finishing in the top half. How would an investor know which of the top first period performers to choose? Making such a choice is the equivalent of flipping a coin.

Even more surprising may be the performance of the first period's bottom quartile performers. These bottom performers had a 50 percent chance of finishing in the *top half* in the succeeding period. Once again, relying on the past performance of actively managed funds has proven to be an unreliable indicator of their future performance. You might as well flip a coin or consult your horoscope.

In his book *A Random Walk Down Wall Street*, Burton Malkiel reported that he did extensive testing on whether an investor, by choosing the "hot" funds, could outperform the market. The results showed the ineffectiveness of a strategy that chose the top 10, 20, 30 or more funds, based on the performance of the previous 12 months, and then one year later switched to the new top performers. Since 1980 this strategy produced results that were not only below the average mutual fund but also below that of the

S & P 500 Index. Similar results were found when Malkiel tried ranking funds by their past two-, five-, and ten-year track records. Furthermore, Malkiel's study ignored all sales commissions, loads, and taxes, which, as I will show, all play a major part in determining after-tax returns, the only kind of returns you can spend. While those who ignore the past may be doomed to repeat it, investors cannot assure themselves of superior performance by relying on funds that have previously beat the market. The following story should help convince you.

The largest mutual funds presumably reached their lofty status because their superior performance continued to attract additional investors. Lipper Analytical Services reported that for the three-year period September 16, 1993–September 19, 1996, not a single one of the 10 largest funds managed to outperform the S & P 500 Index. Notably, the only one that came even close was the passively managed Vanguard Index 500 fund. This fund does not attempt to either pick stocks or time the market; its only objective is to replicate the performance of the S & P 500 Index. As you can see in the table that follows, it gets an A from its investors for doing its job in a very cost-effective manner.

While the Vanguard Index 500 fund was doing its job, the largest fund, the $53 billion Fidelity Magellan, managed to underperform the S & P 500 Index by 450 basis points ($4^{1}/_{2}$ percent) per annum. Two of the ten managed to underperform by about 6 percent per annum. If one excludes the one index fund in the group, the remaining funds, all actively managed, turned in an average performance of 13.91 percent, underperforming their benchmark index by over 3 percent per annum. Investors were paying considerable fees for poor performance. Keep in mind that these returns are pretax. On an after-tax basis the relative performance numbers of the actively managed funds only gets worse.

Active Portfolio Management Is a Loser's Game

Mutual Fund	9/16/93–9/19/96 (Annual Return)
Fidelity Magellan	12.60%
Investment Co. of America	14.24%
Vanguard Index 500	16.95%
Washington Mutual Investors	16.02%
Fidelity Contrafund	15.35%
Fidelity Growth & Income	16.43%
Fidelity Puritan	11.12%
20th Century Ultra	14.49%
Income Fund of America	10.92%
Vanguard Windsor	14.08%
S & P 500 Index	17.10%

Source: Lipper Analytical Services, Inc.

It's also worth noting that over the 5-, 10-, and 15-year periods ending April 30, 1997, the Vanguard Index 500 fund outperformed at least 90 percent of Morningstar's large-cap universe. Noting this performance, *Fortune* magazine asked the question: If indexing works so well with the big U.S. stocks that make up the S & P 500, why not index your whole portfolio?[11] Maybe *Fortune* should take its own advice and stop recommending the "best" or the "hot" funds to buy.

If I have not yet convinced you that "riding" the hot money manager is the losing strategy, an examination of the performance of 1995's top managers in 1996 should do the trick. According to Morningstar's database, while the S & P 500 Index was up more than 20 percent in 1996, the top performing fund from 1995, Alger Capital Appreciation, was up 13.8 percent. The average 1996 performance of 1995's top 10 funds was 5.8 percent. In addition, while only 15 out of over two thousand funds managed to lose money in 1996, four of the previous year's top 10 managed to accomplish that feat. It seems that Wall Street has something in common with Hollywood—sequels are never as good as the originals.

Faced with this evidence, one has to wonder why individual investors continue to pour money into last year's hot performers and other actively managed funds. Could it be that they are not aware of the poor performance of these funds over the long term? Certainly the actively managed funds are not about to tell you of a September 1996 Lipper Analytical Services study that showed the average diversified U.S. mutual fund returned to its investors a 12.1 percent rate of return over the previous 10-year period. Not a bad return, until you compare this performance to that of the S & P 500 Index, which increased at a rate of 13.8 percent per annum.[12]

Chasing the Hot Money Manager

The following is one of my favorite stories about investors believing in both past performance predicting future results and "riding the hot hand." On January 1, 1996, the Van Wagoner Emerging Growth Fund opened its doors to new investors. By late May, the net asset value of the fund had risen an incredible 61 percent for any investor lucky enough to have invested on day one. Most investors in this fund, as I will show, were not so fortunate. Having posted such impressive returns, the fund received a tidal wave of new money. By July 24, the fund's asset base had grown dramatically, but the net asset value of the fund was now only 23 percent above where it had started. Because the fund was so much larger, the May–July decline "not only burned through $90 million in net profits that shareholders had accumulated in the first five months, it also added $80 million in losses. Not surprisingly, investors headed for the exits."[13] Next time you are tempted to invest with the latest hot hand, remember the Van Wagoner story.

Relying on Trade Publications

I call much of the output of Wall Street and the trade publications that cover the financial markets "investment pandering." You may be wondering what pandering has to do with the world of investments. A panderer caters to or profits from the weakness or vices of others. The panderer titillates, stimulates, and excites people into action. The roller-coaster swing of opinions that come from Wall Street, the media, and the trade publications covering the industry, reflects attempts to do just that. Pandering is also exploitative; the investment community is exploiting the individual investor's lack of knowledge. That is why I find "investment pandering" an accurate as well as descriptive term for much of what passes as expert advice. Jane Bryant Quinn, the highly regarded, nationally syndicated columnist, goes even further than I do. She writes:

> Americans are indulging themselves in investment porn. Shameless stories about performance tickle our prurient financial interest.

Then she writes:

> Mainline magazines (like *Money*, *Smart Money*, and *Worth*) . . . rarely descend to hard-core porn. That is what you get from the greedy gurus on cable TV, or the cruising shysters on the Internet. Senator James Exon is wasting his talents trying to vaporize

Internet sex. Let him go after the schmucks who molest your pocketbook by hyping stocks online.

Quinn adds:

We in the quality-media crowd specialize in soft-core porn. . . . *The porn test isn't the headline, but whether the story is anchored in reality.* (Emphasis mine.)

And she concludes:

In this tough and competitive marketplace (of personal finance magazines) publications that merely dispense information will see their readers melt away. Investors want action . . . they want to peep.[14]

Merton Miller, a Nobel laureate, in an interview with *Barron's*, was asked: What advice would you give the average investor? His response: "Don't quote me on this, but I'd say don't read *Barron's*." Why? "Because," he continued, "it will only tease you about investment opportunities that you'd best avoid."[15]

Let's examine why much of the output of Wall Street and the media deserves the name "investment pandering."

The Class of '95

Each year *Business Week* selects "The 100 Best Small Companies." An investor who believes in *Business Week*'s skill in stock selection could build a portfolio of these one hundred great companies. For the two-year period ending April 30, 1997, the Russell 2000 Index, a benchmark for small companies, rose 33 percent. *Business Week* reported that a Class of '95 portfolio would have lost 4.5 percent. An investor believing that *Business Week* somehow possessed more knowledge than the market as a whole underperformed, by 37.5 percent, the return every investor could have achieved simply by buying a Russell 2000 Index fund.[16]

The Class of '91

In case you thought the preceding example was either unique or that two years was too short a time frame, let's examine the *Forbes* Class of '91, *Forbes*'s list of the two hundred best small companies of 1991. Five years later, *Forbes* reported that a portfolio of these companies would have provided a return of 88 percent. Not bad, except that the National Association of Securities Dealers Automated Quotations (NASDAQ) Index rose 140 percent over the same period. In addition, only 44 (22 percent) of the two hundred managed to beat the performance of the NASDAQ.[17] Another benchmark, the passively managed small company asset class fund, as represented by the DFA 9-10 fund, was up 151 percent for the period.

The Best Mutual Funds

At the end of 1994, *Worth* magazine chose the "best" mutual funds, allowing an investor to construct a portfolio consisting of actively managed funds in the five asset classes of global, U.S. large-cap growth, U.S. small-cap growth, U.S. large-cap value, and U.S. small-cap value. The value the active managers would provide could then be measured against an equivalent portfolio of passively managed asset class funds. Dimensional Fund Advisors (DFA) provides a group of passively managed funds that one can use as benchmarks. Four of the five passive funds beat their *Worth* counterparts, with the sole winner, the Heartland Fund, beating its passive counterpart by just 0.5 percent. The combined *Worth* portfolio underperformed by 5.65 percent. With *Worth*'s portfolio adding *negative value*, consumers certainly weren't getting their money's "worth." They should have realized that what they were really buying was "pulp fiction."

Worth Magazine's "Best Mutual Funds" Selected November 1994:
How much value did they add relative to asset class funds in 1995?

Asset Class	Performance 12/31/94–12/31/95	Relative Value Added
"Best Global Equity Fund"		
Worth: Warburg Pincus		
International Equity	+9.85%	
DFA Large Cap International	+13.05%	
DFA International Value	+11.49%	−2.42%
"Best Large Cap Growth Fund"		
Worth: Fidelity Disciplined Equity	+29.01%	
DFA U.S. large company	+37.08%	−8.07%
"Best Small Cap Growth Fund"		
Worth: Wasatch Aggressive Equity	+28.12%	
DFA U.S. 9–10 small	+34.46%	−6.34%
"Best Large Cap Value Fund"		
Worth: Mutual Beacon	+25.89%	
DFA: U. S. large-cap value	+38.36%	−12.47%
"Best Small Cap Value Fund"		
Worth: Heartland Value	+29.80%	
DFA U. S. small-cap value	+29.29%	+0.51%
Worth: equal weighted portfolio	+24.64%	
DFA equal weighted portfolio	+30.29%	−5.65%

The Yanni Bilkey Investment Company provided further evidence against relying on trade magazines in a 1991 study. Each year *Forbes* recommends a "Hall of Fame" list of mutual funds individuals should buy. For the seven five-year periods beginning in 1980, only once, and by the smallest of margins, did the group beat the S & P 500 Index. However, they never once beat the average equity fund. Another study on this famous list covered the period 1983–1990 and found that a portfolio of the Hall of Fame funds would have returned 10.46 percent, versus 16.43 percent for the S & P 500 Index.[18] This list has come to be known as the Hall of Shame list. To be listed is like the kiss of death.

Here is another interesting point. If past performance had predictive value, then *Forbes*'s Hall of Fame would list the same group of funds year after year. Investors should be asking themselves: Why don't the same funds repeat their appearance on the "Best Buy" list? If the same funds don't repeat, how valuable is the list?

One last anecdote on relying on trade publications for advice. The June 1996 issue of *Smart Money* featured their annual Superstar Funds list. In reviewing last year's Superstar selections, reporter Nellie Huang observed that while beating the S & P 500 Index is difficult for active managers, "our eight Superstar Funds have been able to match the surging market, on average, since we picked them. . . . as a group our 1995 Superstars posted an average return of 27.7 percent. That compares with 28.2 percent for the Vanguard 500 Index fund (a passively managed fund) over the same period." Maybe the times they are a-changing. Now a strategy "works" if it only trails the benchmark index by 50 basis points (0.5 percent)!

Undaunted by the failure of its superstar funds to beat the market in 1995, *Smart Money* picked the seven best funds for 1996. The February 1997 issue reported that for the 12-month period ending December 4, 1996, *Smart Money*'s superstar funds were up about 16 percent. Not bad, except that the S & P 500 Index was up almost 28 percent. The superstar funds provided returns that were 12 percent below the return that was available to every investor.

It is also worth noting that the June 1995 issue of *Smart Money* contained the following forecast: "These eight Superstars should be viewed as 'long-term holds.' We believe they form the bedrock of a well diversified portfolio of equity mutual funds." By May 1996 *Smart Money* was already apologizing for the performance of one of its superstar "long-term holds," the Parnassus Fund. "Parnassus's fall [it was down an astonishing 15 percent between July 1995 and March 1996 while the S & P 500 was rising over 20 percent] was one of stunning proportions."

Relying on Market Newsletters

The last several years have seen a proliferation of mutual fund newsletters, which tout their ability to help individual investors choose mutual funds that will outperform the market. Let's check the record. Mark Hulbert, editor of the *Hulbert Financial Digest*, examined the performance of 27 mutual fund portfolios for which he had 10 years of data. During that time, only one of the 27 (3.7 percent) was able to beat the market as measured by the Wilshire 5000 Index, through June 1996. When he studied 106 newsletter portfolios with at least five years of data, he found that just 12 (11.3 percent) had managed to outperform the Wilshire 5000 Index. Not surprisingly, the longer the time frame covered by Hulbert's study, the lower the percentage of newsletters that were able to beat a market benchmark.[19] What is surprising is that despite this poor performance these mutual fund newsletters continue to proliferate in number, providing Hulbert with a market-place for his product, which ranks their performance. He is now tracking 261 of them. Investors should wake up to the fact that newsletters that tout their ability to predict which mutual funds will outperform the market are no more valuable than tout sheets gamblers purchase at the racetrack. While I admire Mr. Hulbert for his integrity, one has to wonder why anyone would buy even his newsletter in the face of his own evidence that mutual fund newsletters are the equivalent of such tout sheets. The tout sheet analogy is appropriate as it supports one of the theses of this book: One of the reasons investors choose the 6 percent solution is that they love to gamble.

Relying on the Rating Services

If relying on past performance or trade publications is not the way to select mutual funds, maybe investors should rely on such professional rating services as the highly regarded Morningstar. Investors who did would have achieved about as much success as the Grinch had in his attempt to steal Christmas. A Lipper Analytical Services study showed that an investor purchasing a portfolio consisting of only Morningstar's five-star funds, for the period 1990–1994, in each year would have failed to beat his portfolio's respective asset classes. John Rekenthaler, editor of *Morningstar Mutual Funds*, admitted that "the connection between past and future performance has not been firmly established by stars, historic star ratings, or any raw data." He did, however, express optimism that the connection will be found. "Just because you can't figure something out does not mean it cannot be done."[20] Amazing!

To be fair, in the December 8, 1995, issue of *Morningstar Mutual Funds* he stated: "We never intended to suggest that the stars could be used to predict short-term returns or to time fund purchases.

They were just a way to sort funds according to past success." He also stated, "[Our] five-star bond funds have posted lower aggregate returns than their peers." Don Phillips, Morningstar's president, was asked: "How should the star system be used by investors?" His response: "*As a way of identifying funds that have had past success.* The stars take into consideration performance, all costs, and risk. And *performance is probably the weakest of the three factors in terms of projecting from the past into the future*" (my emphasis). It is estimated that over 80 percent of new fund purchases are four- or five-star ranked funds. Apparently, not many investors know that Morningstar's star ratings have no predictive value.[21]

Relying on the Experts

We have two classes of forecasters: those who don't know—and those who don't know they don't know.
—John Kenneth Galbraith

It may seem a bit harsh to call the prognostications of such market experts investment pandering. However, these "experts" are dangerous because individual investors take their advice seriously.

Consider the following headlines that appeared in late 1994 and early 1995, just as the U.S. markets were about to soar to record heights. These quotations, from market gurus and widely read publications, all warn investors about the dangers ahead in the coming months. Such forecasts and headlines are dangerous because they cause investors to veer from the academically proven winner's game of buy and hold.

Active Portfolio Management Is a Loser's Game

Followers of Dow Theory Say Something Has to Give

"What I don't understand is why nobody is willing to talk openly about the fact that we're already in a bear market." (Richard Russell, *Dow Theory Letters*)
—*Wall Street Journal,* December 12, 1994, Dow Industrials 3691.11.

One can only conclude that Mr. Russell must have thought a conspiracy existed among investors to only talk in whispers and behind closed doors about the "fact" that we were in a bear market. The bear market that he was talking about proceeded to rally over 4,000 points over the next three years. Russell managed to cause the subscribers to his *Dow Theory Letters* to miss out on the greatest bull market in history.

From the same article:

"Every time you've had this kind of drop in the Transports, you've always had a significant decline in the Industrials." (Tim Hayes, market analyst, Ned Davis Research)

Calvert Strategic Growth Prepares for the Worst

"Every time all five of our indicators turned negative, we had at least a 20 percent decline. Over the last 40 years, it would have worked every time." (Cedd Moses, portfolio manager, Calvert Strategic Growth Fund)
—*Barron's,* April 17, 1995, Dow Industrials 4208.18.

The last two quotations are particularly dangerous examples of investment pandering. At first look, both Mr. Hayes and Mr. Moses seem to make legitimate claims as reliable predictors. It certainly sounds pretty scary: *"every time."* The problem is that investors are generally not aware that if you look hard enough you can always find some correlation that seems to explain, or predict, past behavior. The availability of today's high-speed computers makes this process, called data mining, an easy one. Unfortunately, the identification of patterns that worked in the past does not necessarily provide you with any useful information about stock price movements in the future. As Andrew Lo, a finance professor at MIT, points out: "Given enough time, enough attempts, and enough imagination, almost any pattern can be teased out of any data set."[22]

The stock and bond markets are filled with wrongheaded data mining. David Leinweber, of First Quadrant Corporation, illustrates this point with what he calls "stupid data-miner tricks." Leinweber sifted through a United Nations CD-ROM and discovered that historically, the single best predictor of the S & P 500 Index was butter production in Bangladesh.[23] His example is a perfect illustration of the fact that the mere existence of a correlation does not necessarily give it predictive value. Some logical reason for the correlation to exist is required for it to have credibility. For example, there is a strong and logical correlation between the level of economic activity and the level of interest rates. As economic activity increases, the demand for money, and therefore its price (interest rates), also increases. Investors who were scared off by the types of alarms set off by Mr. Hayes and Mr. Moses missed out on the largest bull market in history.

Stock Gains Fly in the Face of Convention

"There is great risk in the stock market. I just don't think investors are paying attention." (Geraldine Weiss, editor, *Investment Quality Trends*)
—*USA Today,* May 2, 1995, Dow Industrials 4316.08.

Active Portfolio Management Is a Loser's Game

Did Ms. Weiss think that all investors had gone to sleep? If you read such stories in the right light, you can find them entertaining; just don't rely on these market gurus for your financial advice.

A valuable lesson can also be learned from Michael Berry, manager of Heartland Mid Cap Value Fund, who ruefully claims credit for calling the bottom of the February–April 1997 market tumble. In a speech on April 25, 1997, he declared that a bear market had begun; he then watched with chagrin as the market immediately began one of its greatest bull runs ever.[24]

Possibly the most dramatic and humorous example of the danger of heeding the forecasts of experts was an interview by Joe Kernen of CNBC with Michael Metz of Oppenheimer, a highly regarded Wall Street veteran. When Mr. Metz speaks, people (unfortunately) listen, because what he says appears to make sense. I often have to remind myself to ignore what appears on the surface to be intelligent advice. On Friday, June 20, 1997, the DJIA set an all-time high, closing at 7796. On Monday, the DJIA experienced one of its worst days ever, dropping almost 200 points. When asked by Mr. Kernen for his view, given the preceding day's debacle, he responded: "I'm bearish." Mr. Kernen then reminded Mr. Metz that he had been bearish for several years (and about 4000 points). Mr. Metz then responded: "I'm even more bearish now." Mr. Kernen's response was perfect, and went something like this: "I guess if you were bearish at 3800, you should be more bearish at 7800. Eventually you'll get it right." (Postscript: By July 3, the DJIA had made a new all-time high.) Maybe the type of forecast made by experts such as Mr. Metz should be required to carry a warning from the surgeon general: "This forecast may be dangerous to your financial well-being." Investment advisor John Merrill suggests the following alternatives:

The views expressed are the views of our guest and not of this network. They may be unfounded, biased, self-serving, and completely at odds with your long-term investment success. No due diligence on all past recommendations has been attempted.

Or:

Warning!! The following market analysis will likely be hazardous to your long-term investment strategy if acted upon. It is designed to motivate you to be a short-term trader (most of whom eventually fail) instead of a long-term investor (most of whom succeed).[25]

Investors who follow the dire warnings of the so-called experts are heeding the adage, Better safe than sorry. Unfortunately, they usually end up safe and sorry. Peter Lynch put it this way: "Far more money has been lost by investors in preparing for corrections, or anticipating corrections, than has been lost in the corrections themselves."[26] You can benefit from this book by applying one key principle: Don't trust anybody who thinks they know more than the markets. Instead, trust the markets themselves. Invest whenever you have available funds, stay invested, and, most important, ignore the dire warnings of the so-called experts.

The Royalty of Portfolio Management

In his book *How To Pick Stocks*, Fred Frailey, the deputy editor of *Kiplinger's Personal Finance* magazine offers a series of "insightful interviews with leading mutual fund managers"—the so-called legendary market gurus. Kiplinger himself, in an introduction to the book, calls them the "royalty of portfolio management." What I find most interesting are his commentaries, which follow each interview. Examples follow.

On Mario Gabelli: "The flagship Asset and Value funds did okay (in 1995), but not spectacularly, producing returns of almost 30 percent." Unfortunately, the S & P 500 Index was up over 37 percent, and the large value index was up over 38 percent. In fact, the performance of Gabelli Asset has been so poor, underperforming the S & P 500 in six of the last eight years, that the April 28, 1997 edition of *Fortune* carried this headline: "Super Mario's Super Slump."

On John Neff: "Neff confessed to some disappointment. . . . The Vanguard Windsor Fund matched the S & P 500 in 1994 and trailed the index by 7 percent in 1995."

On Kent Simmons and Larry Marx: "Whatever else you can say of 1996, it was not a Marx-and-Simmons kind of year. By November, Guardian's year-to-date return had crept up to 13 percent—not bad in itself, but still far short of the S & P 500 Index, which was up almost 20 percent."

On Larry Auriana and Hans Utsch: "Kaufman fund returned 37 percent in 1995." Of course this trailed the S & P 500. "Alas, 1996 was another story altogether. Kaufman shot out of the starting gate like a bullet. But it was caught by the mid-year crash of high tech stocks and trailed the S & P 500 thereafter."

On Robert Bacarella: "Moneta perked up in 1995, ultimately returning 28 percent to the S & P 500's 38 percent." This marked "four straight years of underperforming the S & P 500 Index."

On Elizabeth Bramwell: "It's a pity that 1996 ultimately disappointed Bramwell's investors (Bramwell Growth). The fund trailed the S & P 500 substantially."

James Craig (Janus Fund) said: "I need a big year. I'm paid on performance and I haven't had a bonus since 1991."

On James Stowers III (Twentieth Century): "The fund laid a

goose egg. Both funds ended November with returns in single digits—this when the overall market was up by 25 percent."

On Ralph Wagner (Acorn Fund): "Its 1994 total return was −7.5 percent, when most small-company growth funds had about broken even. Then in 1995 it returned 21 percent, or 17 percent lower than the S & P 500 Index."

On Jerome Dodson: "For all of 1995—the best year for stocks in more than three decades—Parnassus merely broke even, returning less than 1 percent. The substandard performance continued throughout 1996. It was as if Dodson had steered his fund into a tree."

On Brad Lewis: "Disciplined Equity's new brain seemed to suffer memory lapse. For the year 1995, the fund trailed by more than 8 percent. In 1996, the shortfall was another 2 percent."

There were many other similar tales. Keep in mind that these quotes are from the very author who not only chose these experts as the royalty of fund managers, but also is the deputy editor of a magazine that recommends to investors which funds should receive their investment dollars.

Even the Best Can't Win the Game

You would think that if anyone could beat the market, it would be the pension funds of the largest U.S companies. After all, they have access to the best and brightest portfolio managers, all of whom are clamoring to manage the billions of dollars in these plans. Presumably, these pension funds rely on the excellent past track records of the "experts" they eventually choose to manage their portfolios.

In a study covering the period 1987–1993, only one out of 28 major pension funds managed to beat a portfolio consisting of a simple 60 percent/40 percent mix of the S & P 500 Index and the Lehman Bond Index, respectively. A 60 percent equity/40 percent fixed income allocation was used, since that is estimated to be the average allocation of all pension plans. The lone fund that did manage to beat the 60/40 fund did so by the slimmest of margins.

Most impressive, however, is that *none* of the funds managed to beat a similar 60/40 model portfolio developed using the Nobel Prize–winning, passive asset class strategy called Modern Portfolio Theory. Unlike the S & P 500 Index portfolio, the Modern Portfolio Theory portfolio is a globally diverse portfolio that invests in the higher risk, and therefore higher yielding, asset classes of value and small companies. (See Exhibit A, page 240.) (How risk affects returns, and how to put the power of Modern Portfolio Theory to work for you, will be addressed in later chapters.)

An updated version of this study, covering 45 companies and the period 1987–1995, found that only five (11 percent) of the pension plans beat the 60/40 benchmark portfolio, and only three (7 percent) beat the portfolio based on Modern Portfolio Theory.

Philip Halpern, the chief investment officer of the Washington State Investment Board (a very large institutional investor) and two of his coworkers wrote an article on their investment experiences. They wrote the article because their experience with active management was less than satisfactory and they knew, through their attendance at professional associations, that many of their colleagues shared, and therefore corroborated, their own experience. They also cited as a reason for writing the article academic research, including a 1995 study done by Kahn and Rudd that concluded that no persistence of returns could be found among U. S. equity managers. They added one other quote from a Goldman Sachs publication: "Few managers consistently outperform the S & P 500. Thus, in the eyes of the plan sponsor, its plan is paying an excessive amount of the upside to the manager while still bearing substantial risk that its investments will achieve sub-par returns." The article concluded, "Slowly, over time, many large pension funds have shared our experience and have moved toward indexing more domestic equity assets."[27]

Jonathan Clements, a columnist for the *Wall Street Journal*, said it best: "I believe the search for top-performing stock funds is an intellectually discredited exercise that will come to be viewed as one of the great financial follies of the late twentieth century."[28]

Ignorance Is Bliss

In the face of this tremendous and ever-mounting body of evidence, why do investors continue to pour their hard-earned investment dollars into actively managed funds? The answer is simple: It certainly isn't in the interest of active managers to inform investors that there is a better way when they are deriving huge fees for producing negative results compared to their benchmarks. Patrick Regnier, associate editor of *Morningstar Investor* magazine, said: "Mutual fund fees are unconscionably high. They get higher every year, while funds get bigger every year—and that should make the fees smaller"—by virtue of the economies of scale.[29] And, as Rex Sinquefield of DFA says, "We all know that active management fees are high. Poor performance does not come cheap. You have to pay dearly for it." In the investment business, while investors don't always get what they pay for, they always pay for what they get.

Whose Interests Do They Have At Heart?

Jean Baptiste Colbert, finance minister to Louis XIV, summed up his views on taxation with the following: "The art of taxation consists in so plucking the goose as to obtain the largest possible amount of feathers with the least possible amount of hissing." The same can be said of active managers—they want to keep plucking those large management fees from the pockets of individual investors with the least possible amount of hissing. In order to continue doing so, they must keep alive the myth that active management works. Frank Knight, a professor of economics at the University of Chicago from 1928 until his death in 1972 at the age of 87, said it best when he claimed that economic theory was not at all obscure or complicated, but that most people had a vested interest in refusing to recognize what was "insultingly obvious."[30]

If you believe that Wall Street places your interests at the top of its priorities, the following excerpt from an internal memo of a large brokerage firm disseminated to its sales force should convince you otherwise. I have omitted the name of the firm, not to protect the guilty but because the memo could just as easily have come from any other firm. The memo was in response to requests from its sales force for the firm to offer index funds. The sales force was simply responding to similar requests from clients who had heard about the superior performance of these passively managed funds.

> Index funds are passively managed mutual funds. They simply buy and hold all the stocks of a popular index such as the Standard and Poor's 500. . . . Because their turnover is low and they don't require large research staffs, most have low operating expenses. . . . The performance of an index fund is a function of two

factors; the performance of the index itself, and the fees to operate and DISTRIBUTE the fund. *For a fund to be successful in the brokerage community it must adequately compensate brokers through either an up-front commission or an ongoing service fee. As a result, a broker-sold index fund would underperform no-load index funds. This is why most index funds are offered by no-load fund groups"* (emphasis mine).

Index funds are not sold by brokers because they do not perform well. They are not sold because investors can buy them cheaper elsewhere. In addition, there is just not enough revenue available to compensate the broker, whose first priority is generating fees, not obtaining the best possible results for his or her clients. In other words, mutual fund sponsors avoid indexing because, while the record makes clear that it is the winning strategy for investors, it is not very profitable for fund sponsors. They see indexing as the losing business strategy.

For these reasons Wall Street does not educate consumers about the virtues of passive management and continues to extol the dubious virtues of active management. It is clearly in the interests of Wall Street to charge you 1.5 percent for an underperforming actively managed fund rather than 0.25 percent to 0.5 percent for a passively managed fund with superior performance.

Nor is it in the interests of the trade magazines and publications to inform investors of what is in their best interests. If they simply offered you the information provided in this book, who would buy their publications? And what would happen to all those market gurus who appear on CNBC and CNN if everyone regarded them as investment panderers?

That Giant Sucking Sound

Individual investors have not been totally blind to the underperformance of active managers. That giant sucking sound you've been hearing recently isn't the sound of jobs disappearing as Ross Perot predicted with the passage of NAFTA; it is the sound of money being siphoned out of actively managed funds and into passively managed funds. "The reason for the stampede couldn't be clearer: the S & P 500 Index has walloped the stock pickers. During the past two years the average equity fund has underperformed the S & P 500 Index by a cumulative 13 percent. Over the past 10 years the average equity fund has underperformed the S & P benchmark by almost 2 percent per annum."[31]

Believers in active management are left with believing that they will make up for their underperformance in bull markets with superior performance in bear markets. Susan Byrne, of the Westwood Equity fund, when asked by *Fortune* magazine about index funds, responded: "An index fund . . . doesn't have a conscience. It doesn't think. That's how you get overvalued stocks. . . . The reason index funds are beating everybody is that the market has been going straight up. When we are not in a straight-up market everyone will beat them."[32] Let's look at the record. "In the market correction of mid-1990, when the S & P 500 fell 14.7 percent, actively managed funds fell an average of 17.9 percent. In 1994, when the Index posted a tiny 1.3 percent gain, the active managers lost 1.4 percent."[33] We are left wondering: exactly when do investors in actively managed funds get rewarded for their faith in the skills of stock pickers and market timers?

The Competition Is Too Tough

Academics would say that "experts" cannot beat the market because it is "efficient" (a term I will explain later). A less technical way of saying the same thing (and also explaining why hard work is not its own reward) is that there are so many bright, hard-working individuals trying to beat the market that the competition is awfully tough. Benjamin Graham, undoubtedly our most famous author on security analysis (legendary investor Warren Buffett is an almost religious devotee of Graham) felt that the results of security analysts depended more on the level of their competition than on the level of their skill. The tougher the competition, the tougher it is to beat the market. Today, over 80 percent of all trading is done by institutional investors. Charles Ellis notes: "Half of all trading on the NYSE is done by the 50 most active institutional investors, . . . all of which are fully staffed by the very best people available. Every investor in the market is competing with these giants all the time."[34] In order to win this game you have to believe that others are making mistakes in how they price securities. In other words, everyone else is wrong, and you are right.

Burton Malkiel provides the following insight:

> Stock trading among institutional investors [because they are the market] is like isometric exercise: lots of energy is expended, but between one investment manager and another it all balances out, and the commissions the managers pay [as well as the other expenses they incur] detract from performance. Like greyhounds at the race track, professional money managers seem destined to lose their race with the mechanical rabbit.[35]

(I have taken the liberty of adding my thoughts to Malkiel's excellent analogy.)

Being Smart Is Not Good Enough

When I was a child we played with a very popular device known as Chinese Handcuffs. It was a cylindrical device, about six inches long, into which you inserted the forefinger of each hand. Once your fingers were inside the bamboo cylinder, you were instructed to try to remove them. As the effort expended in pulling your fingers apart increased, the bamboo cylinder tightened, and your fingers were even more entrapped. Active management is a lot like Chinese Handcuffs. The greater the effort expended, the more entrapped you become in a losing struggle.

Active managers must be smarter than the market, because the very act of active management, with all the research and trading expenses incurred, puts them at a disadvantage relative to passive managers. Let's examine why the impact of expenses and taxes makes active management a losing game.

As mentioned earlier, the average actively managed equity mutual fund has research and operating expenses of about 1.5 percent, compared with expenses of about 0.25 percent to 0.50 percent for passively managed funds, such as index funds, which avoid the research expenses that active managers incur. Thus, passively managed funds have an immediate advantage of 1 percent to 1.25 percent over actively managed funds. Who bears the greater costs of the actively managed funds? Investors do, in the form of reduced returns.

Given the poor performance of actively managed funds, you might ask, How do they get away with such high fees? It's simple: Investors let them. Amy Arnott of Morningstar provides a good explanation for this seemingly irrational behavior. "People haven't focused on costs, because the markets have done so well in recent years. It's also because investors don't receive a bill from the fund labeled 'management fee.' The money is simply deducted from the fund's total assets, so it never shows up on an account statement."[36]

Given the total indifference shown by shareholders, it's hardly surprising that fees have remained stubbornly high; what is amazing is the twisted logic that funds use to justify a raise even after years of poor performance. Take Seligman Income, which produced only two-thirds of the average returns of similar funds for the years 1994–1995. Despite the poor performance, the board proposed raising fees by 22 percent. Its explanation: "to remain competitive and invest in people and resources necessary to continue to provide a high level of service." In 1996 the fund provided a return of only 8.22 percent versus the 13.34 percent produced by its peers. One can only imagine how badly the fund would have done without the extra help.[37]

Trading Expenses

Mutual funds must absorb the difference between the bid (the price at which traders will buy) and the offer (the price at which traders will sell) on all their trades. Each time a security is purchased they must pay the offer price, while each time they sell a security they only receive the bid price. Passively managed funds, because they trade infrequently, have low trading costs. Actively managed funds, by definition, trade more often and therefore incur the cost of the bid-offer spread more frequently. (I will explore in a later chapter just how big a hurdle trading activity creates for actively managed funds in their attempt to beat the market.)

Tax Burden

Finally, active managers must overcome the burden of the tax consequences of their trading activity. Internal Revenue Service (IRS) regulations require mutual funds to distribute at least 98 percent of their realized income in order to maintain their tax-exempt status. (If a fund does not meet this requirement it is subject to an excise tax of 4 percent.) The typical actively managed fund turns over, or replaces, about 80 percent of the stocks in its portfolio each year. The result is that the fund actually realizes gains, as opposed to just reporting an increase in the value of the portfolio, and investors pay both ordinary income and capital gains taxes on those distributions.

It is important to note that a direct correlation between turnover and distributions does not exist. Higher turnover doesn't necessarily, at least in the short term, translate into greater capital gains distributions. As individual investors have become more aware of the impact of taxes on their investment returns, some fund managers have begun to try to manage taxes in a more effective manner. When the turnover of actively managed funds results in realized gains, the fund manager may then sell securities that will generate an offsetting loss. While this strategy may reduce taxes in the short term, the increased turnover caused by the activity, known as harvesting of losses, results in increased trading expenses and lower returns.

Consider this example. In 1995, a terrific year for the U. S. markets, many equity mutual funds were able to report gains of 30 percent or more. An individual who had invested $1,000 in an actively managed fund, with an 80 percent turnover rate and a 30 percent rise in the value of its portfolio (to $1,300), might have received a year-end distribution of $240 ($1,000 × 30 percent × 80 percent). A portion of this distribution is likely to be taxed as ordinary income, with the balance taxed at the preferential capital gains rate. If one assumes an average tax rate (both state and federal) of 35 percent, the investor would incur $84 in income taxes, leaving only $156 to reinvest, not the original $240. The investor would begin the next year with $1,216 ($1,300 − $84), not $1,300. In advertising its annual rate of return, a mutual fund assumes you are able to reinvest the full $1,300, not $1,216 (which would only be true if the fund was held in a tax-deferred account).

The typical passively managed fund has a much lower turnover rate than an actively managed fund. Depending on the asset class, a passive fund may have turnover of as little as 1–2 percent, or as high as 20–25 percent. The turnover of passively managed funds is generated by acquisitions—and by the price performance of individual securities, which causes them to move in or out of the asset class the passive fund represents, as when a small company grows to be a large company. A small company fund then has to sell the shares of that company, or the fund loses its pure asset class status as a small company fund. If a passively managed fund had turnover of 10 percent, an investor, on average, would only pay current income taxes on 10 percent of the fund's appreciation while being able to defer income taxes on the remaining 90 percent.

Returning to our earlier example, an individual with $1,000 in a passively managed fund with a 10 percent turnover rate of its portfolio, and the same 30 percent increase in the value of the fund, might have received a distribution of $30 (as compared to $240), and paid taxes of about $12 (as compared to $84). This investor would begin the following year with $1,288 (as compared to $1,216. Despite the identical pretax performance of the investments, the investor in the passively managed fund begins the new year with an extra $72. This differential will provide dramatic differences in returns, as I will show, over long periods of time.

Most investors, because of Wall Street's heavy promotion of IRAs, are well informed about the benefits of deferring income taxes. Ironically, while Wall Street educates investors on the tax benefits of IRAs, investors are kept in the dark about the tax effects of active management.

Although the effect of paying current income taxes may be minimal (and therefore insidious) in any one year, it is dramatic over a protracted period of time. A recent study commissioned by Charles Schwab and conducted by John Shoven, a Stanford University professor of economics, and Joel Dickson, a Stanford Ph.D. candidate, demonstrated just how great an effect this stealth attack produced on returns. The study measured the performance of 62 equity funds for the 30-year period 1963–1992 and found that while each dollar invested in this group of funds would have grown to $21.89 in a tax-deferred account, the same amount of money invested in a taxable account would have produced only $9.87 for a high–tax bracket investor. Amazingly, and painfully, taxes cut returns by 57.5 percent.[38]

Further evidence on the effect of taxes on returns comes from a study covering the five-year period 1992–1996. According to Morningstar, diversified U. S. stock funds gained an average of 91.9 percent over the period. Morningstar then assumed that income and short-term gains were taxed at 39.6 percent and long-term capital gains at 28 percent. The result was that after-tax returns dwindled to 71.5 percent, a loss of 23 percent of the returns in just five years.[39]

Passively managed funds are not as tax efficient as a tax-deferred account. However, because of their high tax efficiency, they are the next best thing. Because of its lower turnover, a passively managed fund would have produced a return much closer to the pretax figure, in the example, of $21.89.

To see how taxes impact the current rate of return, let's look at two hypothetical funds, one actively managed, the other passively managed. Assume that both achieved a total return of 12 percent, resulting from a 2 percent return from dividends and a 10 percent return from capital gains. Assume also that the actively managed fund had a turnover rate of 80 percent, while the passively managed fund had a turnover rate of 10 percent. These are fairly representative turnover rates. The realized gains figure is obtained by multiplying the turnover rate by the amount of capital gains. Here's how returns were affected by the difference in turnover:

Assumptions	Actively Managed	Passively Managed
Dividends	2.0% (a)	2.0% (a)
Realized gains	8.0% (b)	1.0% (b)
Unrealized gains	2.0%	9.0%
Total return	**12.0% (c)**	**12.0% (c)**
Ordinary tax rate	40.0% (d)	40.0% (d)
Capital gains rate	30.0% (e)	30.0% (e)
Ordinary tax (axd)	0.8% (f)	0.8% (f)
Capital gains tax (bxe)	2.4% (g)	0.3% (g)
Total tax (f + g)	**3.2% (h)**	**1.1% (h)**
Current after-tax return (c − h)	8.8%	10.9%

The higher turnover of the actively managed fund had a dramatic negative impact on the current after-tax return. Because a significant portion of distributed capital gains is likely to be short-term (particularly for an actively managed fund), and therefore taxed at ordinary income tax rates (instead of the lower capital gains rate), the tax impact would be even greater than that shown in the table. Now you can see why actively managed mutual funds do not like to discuss their turnover rates, or the resulting tax impact.

Robert Jeffrey and Robert Arnott also demonstrated the effects of taxes' "stealth attack" on returns when they studied the performance of 72 actively managed funds for the period 1982–1991. They found that while 15 of the 72 funds beat a passively managed fund on a pretax basis, only five did so on an after-tax basis.[40]

Another tax-related problem with actively managed mutual funds is that their distributions are unpredictable. An investor may decide to purchase a fund because in the past it has made very small distributions (is tax efficient). Unfortunately, a history of low distributions is not a good predictor of future distributions. An active manager may decide to take profits on securities that have been held for a very long time and have a very low cost basis. The distribution caused by realizing that profit would lead to a large, and unanticipated, tax bill. Worse yet, if an investor purchased shares in the mutual fund shortly before the distribution date, he or she would have had to pay taxes on profits from which he or she never benefited.

Fund distributions, and their effect on returns in taxable accounts, can be sizable. *Bloomberg Business News* reported that the largest distribution ever in dollar terms, $13.35 per share, was paid out in May 1996 by Fidelity's Magellan Fund. This distribution was related to gains the fund made between November 1, 1995, and March 31, 1996. Fidelity's management stated that most of the gains were made in late 1995, when former manager Jeffrey Vinik sold off "a significant number of technology stocks." Pity the unwary investors who purchased shares in Fidelity Magellan in April 1996. Without benefiting from any of the prior profits, they faced a tax bill on the largest distribution ever made. With active managers, you never know when unrealized gains will be realized. Passively managed funds will always have relatively low turnover, making their distributions far more predictable.

Summary

Peter Bernstein, the founder of the *Journal of Portfolio Management*, said: "The essence of investment theory is that being smart is not a sufficient condition for being rich."[41] He was right. As I have shown, being smart is not enough to beat the market. The research and trading expenses and the tax consequences of active managers giving it the "old college try" create hurdles that are just too great to overcome. I hope that all this evidence has convinced you that active management is a loser's game. It certainly convinced the American Law Institute:

The Prudent Investor Rule

There are well-dressed foolish ideas just as there are well-dressed fools. —Nicholas Chamfort

Embedded within the American legal code is a doctrine known as the Prudent Investor Rule. Basically, this rule states that if you are responsible for the management of someone else's assets, you must manage those assets as would a prudent investor. For example, if you are the trustee of the assets of an elderly widow you should be investing her money in safe assets, not in a commodity trading account. At one time, stocks were considered so risky that trustees considered bonds the only appropriate investments; even corporate pension funds reflected that view. That attitude has changed, and it is now generally recognized that equities are risky only if the investment time horizon is short. The average U. S. pension fund now has an equity asset allocation of about 60 percent.

During the 1970s, pension fund administrators began to discern that the collective performance of the active managers they hired to manage their pension fund assets was poor. This realization created the initial demand for the creation of index funds. Even though a few index funds became available, it wasn't until 1990, and the awarding of the Nobel Prize to Miller, Sharpe, and Markowitz, that the benefits of Modern Portfolio Theory became more widely known.

Around May 1992, in response to both the overwhelming body of academic evidence about the overall unsatisfactory performance of active managers and the benefits of passive asset class investing, the American Law Institute rewrote the Prudent Investor Rule. Here is a summary of what the Institute had to say in doing so:

- The restatement's objective is to liberate expert trustees to pursue challenging, rewarding, nontraditional strategies and to provide other trustees with clear guidance to safe harbors that are practical and expectedly rewarding.

- Investing in index funds is a passive but practical investment alternative.

- Risk may be reduced by mixing risky assets with essentially riskless assets, rather than by creating an entirely low-risk portfolio.

- *Active strategies entail investigation and expenses that increase transaction costs, including capital gains taxation.* Proceeding with such a program involves judgments by the trustee that gains from the course of action in question can reasonably be expected to *compensate for additional cost and risks,* and the course of action to be *undertaken is reasonable in terms of its economic rationale.*

By rewriting the Prudent Investor Rule, the American Law Institute recognized both the significance and efficacy of Modern Portfolio Theory and that active management delivers inconsistent and poor results. The Institute had the following to say about market efficiency, in summary:

- Economic evidence shows that the major capital markets of this country are *highly efficient*, in the sense that available information is rapidly digested and reflected in market prices.

- Fiduciaries and other investors are confronted with potent evidence that the application of expertise, investigation, and diligence in efforts to "beat the market" ordinarily promises little or no payoff, or even a negative payoff after taking account of research and transaction costs.

- Empirical research supporting the theory of efficient markets reveals that in such markets skilled professionals have rarely been able to identify underpriced securities with any regularity.

- Evidence shows that there is little correlation between fund managers' earlier successes and their ability to produce above-market returns in subsequent periods.

Two states, New York and Pennsylvania, have already passed legislation with two major revisions to the Prudent Investor Rule:

- Modern Portfolio Theory is adopted as the standard by which fiduciaries invest funds.

- Fiduciaries can avoid liability if they exercise reasonable skill and care in making a delegation to an agent. The agent will be held to the same standards as the fiduciary.

The same legislation is now working its way through the legislatures of other states.[42]

For those with fiduciary responsibility, adopting Modern Portfolio Theory makes sense because:

- It can provide the maximum expected return for a given level of risk.

- It provides relief from liability for fiduciaries who are not in the investment business by appointing competent managers or advisors who invest according to its tenets.

Faced with this restatement, and the recent legislative changes, trustees began a major switch from active to passive portfolio strategies. As recently as 15 years ago, around $1 billion was invested in passive funds. Today the amount invested is over $1 trillion and may represent as much as 40 percent of institutional funds (i.e., pension plans and endowment funds). In fact, the largest U.S. investment fund, the almost $100 billion CREF stock account (Teacher's Insurance and Annuity Association Retirement Equities Fund) indexes about 70 percent of the fund's assets.[43] One reason for this rapid shift is that pension fund managers must now ask themselves: "Do I want to invest in a way that has been awarded a Nobel Prize, and has been recognized as prudent by the American Law Institute? Or would I rather try, with historical evidence against me, to beat the market through an active management strategy, knowing that if I fail I may be forced to justify why I took such a strategy in the face of an overwhelming body of academic evidence?" Consider this baseball analogy. The score is tied in the bottom of the ninth. The lead-off runner singles. Not wanting to be second-guessed in the light of all the historical evidence, the manager will probably "play it by the book" and attempt to bunt the runner into scoring position. Like the baseball manager, institutional fund managers and other trustees are faced with a wealth of historical evidence that is leading them to play it by the book. Given the risk/reward trade-off, I believe that the growing trend toward the use of passive asset class investing by institutional investors is not only inevitable but will accelerate.

Evidence of this trend came when *Institutional Investor* magazine declared 1997 "the year of the passive manager" in their nineteenth Pension Olympics. Passive managers not only racked up the largest gains as a group, but passive houses took both the silver and gold medals for gaining the most institutional assets. The magazine attributed the large gains made by the two firms to "the accelerating search by pension funds for consistent performance." Frederick Grauer, cochairman of Barclays Global Investors, the world's largest institutional fund manager, noted that "there are trends that have been major market drivers for the decade. Indexing people are looking to reduce costs, control exposures to the marketplace and to get exact implementation of pension policies. They are fed up with out-of-control outcomes."[44]

The trend to passive investing is not only apparent in the institutional market, but is also rapidly gaining momentum in the retail market as well. It took Vanguard, by far the largest provider of retail-oriented passively managed funds, eleven years (1976–1987) to attract its first $1 billion to its S & P 500 Index fund. In early 1997 it crossed $30 billion and, incredibly, by midyear had crossed $40 billion. While active managers will probably never go the way of buggy whip manufacturers, their market share will inevitably decline.

Filling In the Void

The balance of this book will provide you with a theoretical understanding of both the interaction between risk and return and how markets work. Having seen how markets work, you will have the skills to make them work for you. You will see that active management does not make sense theoretically and is not justified empirically.

When you complete this book, you will be able to emulate the Nobel Prize–winning strategy used by the most knowledgeable institutions. It will no longer be necessary for you to watch CNBC, read *Money* magazine, or spend time analyzing investment advice from your broker, who only makes money when you trade, whether or not the trade was in your best interest. You will begin to let the markets work for you. Instead of listening to the latest hot tip from your friend, broker, or barber, you will be investing in a way recommended by the brightest academic minds in the field of economics. It should comfort you to know that your investment strategy is based on research that was awarded a Nobel Prize. Your newly acquired knowledge will allow you to play the winner's game of managing returns by managing risks. You will no longer play the loser's game of trying to pick stocks and time the market. Finally, since the ultimate objective of investing is consumption, you will probably eat a lot better, too. Wouldn't that make a pretty good story to tell at the next cocktail party you attend? In fact, instead of having that one great cocktail party story to tell, you will be the one throwing the party.

PART TWO

◆

EFFICIENT MARKETS
AND MODERN
PORTFOLIO THEORY

I am no longer an advocate of elaborate techniques of security analysis in order to find superior value opportunities. This was a rewarding activity, say forty years ago, when Graham and Dodd was first published; but the situation has changed.... [Today] I doubt whether such extensive efforts will generate sufficiently superior selections to justify their cost.... I'm on the side of the "efficient" market school of thought.
—Benjamin Graham, the father of fundamental security analysis (the art of trying to identify securities that the rest of the market has mispriced, or undervalued) in an interview in the *Financial Analysts Journal* shortly before his death in 1976, quoted in *A Random Walk Down Wall Street* by Burton G. Malkiel

◆

It isn't what people think that is important, but the reason they think what they think. —Eugene Ionesco

◆

There is only one good, knowledge, and one evil, ignorance.
—Plato

◆

Even if you identify the managers who have good past performance, there's no guarantee that they'll have good future performance. —George Sauter, Vanguard Group

CHAPTER 3

◆

Efficient Markets I—
Information and Costs

There is one thing stronger than all the armies in the world, and that is an idea whose time has come. —Victor Hugo

Only liars manage to always be out during bad times and in during good times. —Bernard Baruch

The evidence clearly indicates that active managers as a group produce results that are consistently below that of their benchmarks, such as the S & P 500. In addition, just as in Las Vegas— where the longer gamblers stay at the tables, the smaller the number of winners—the longer the investment horizon, the lower the percentage of active managers who manage to beat their benchmarks. According to one school of economists, the efficient markets theory explains this phenomenon; this theory argues that current market prices reflect the total knowledge and expectations of all investors, and no one investor can know more than the market does collectively. For this theory to hold true, one condition must be met: Any new information must be disseminated to the public rapidly and completely so that prices instantly adjust to new data. If this is the case, an investor can consistently beat the market only with the best of luck.

While the information condition is at the core of the efficient market theory, there are two other factors related to market efficiency that affect the development of a winning investment strategy: cost and risk.

If the investor's cost to enter into a market transaction is relatively low, the market can be considered efficient from a *cost* perspective, and the trading costs incurred by active management are relatively low. The more inefficient the market (the greater the spread between the bid and offer), however, the greater are both the costs of trading and the barriers that active managers must hurdle in order to beat their benchmarks.

Market efficiency must also be considered from a *risk* perspective. In brief: Do investments that entail greater risk provide investors with greater returns as compensation for the greater risk assumed?

Once you have a grasp of these three elements of market efficiency—information, cost, and risk—you will realize not only why active management is a loser's game but, more important, why Modern Portfolio Theory provides the winning investment strategy.

This chapter addresses the information and the cost components of efficient markets; the next chapter addresses the risk component.

Efficient Markets and Information

One of my favorite films is *The House of Rothschild*, with George Arliss playing the role of the patriarch of the family. In the film's climactic scene, he has placed his entire family fortune on the line in an attempt to save the British financial system. There is a tidal wave of selling, with shares being dumped at any price, as British traders are anticipating a Napoleonic victory.

Just as the great resources of the House of Rothschild are about to be exhausted, Arliss demands the attention of all the traders, announcing that Wellington is victorious. The traders mock him, saying that he is just trying to save his own fortune with this false rumor. At this point he must disclose the great family secret. (One reason the Rothschilds were able to amass their fortune was that they always were a step ahead of the public in terms of information.) While the fastest ships in the British fleet are just beginning to sail with the news of Napoleon's defeat, carrier pigeons have already delivered the news into Rothschild's hands. With this disclosure, prices soar, and the Rothschilds emerge richer than ever.

Today, Rothschild's advantage is not possible, as information is carried all over the globe in seconds, and markets adjust to news almost instantaneously.

An efficient market exists when trading systems fail to produce returns in excess of the market's overall rate of return, because stocks are already trading at what they are worth, based on all available information. When a market is efficient, information moves rapidly, prices immediately reflect new information, and no investor can consistently know more about an individual security than does the market as a whole. If this is true, then the only way individual stock selection can be productive is if an individual possesses insider information, that is, facts and figures about a company that should only be known by its board of directors, officers, and, perhaps, key upper-level managers. To trade on such privileged information is a violation of the securities laws of the United States.

Institutions Are Now the Market

Over 80 percent of all trading is now done by institutional investors such as mutual funds and pension funds. The managers of these funds—who, as mentioned earlier, are highly paid, intelligent, hard-working individuals—spend a considerable amount of time doing research, mainly to discover securities that they assume have somehow been mispriced by all their equally intelligent and just as hard-working competitors. And all this research incurs lots of expenses (including transaction costs and taxes). Not only do such efforts seem illogical and futile in this light, but study after study has confirmed that they fail. (In fact, not a single credible academic study, of which I am aware, says that active management works; in chapter 9 I show why some studies are not credible because of what is called survivorship bias.) Efforts to beat the market are counterproductive—not because of poor research, but because the research is done so well, by so many people, that no one individual is likely to gain an advantage over another. Therefore, the costs of research are unlikely to be recouped through improved returns.

Binkley Shorts, a portfolio manager at Wellington Management, put it this way: "When you're looking at companies like Microsoft, IBM, Merck, and Coca-Cola, the ability to capture incremental insight is so damn challenging because so many people are looking at those stocks and it takes so long to get through the body of knowledge."[45] The remainder of this section provides evidence that active managers have great difficulty beating the market.

A condition of an efficient market is that information rapidly spreads. With all of the business news sources available today, and the use of the Internet, I don't think anyone would even begin to question whether information travels around the globe in anything except a very rapid manner.

If new information entered into the market slowly, prices would slowly adjust to it. Those receiving it first could profit by acting before the rest of the investing community gained access to it. Markets do not operate this way these days. Today, the price of a company's stock may rise or fall by as much as 20–40 percent immediately after the release of key information—such as its quarterly earnings report or the gain or loss of significant contracts. How fast can the market process new information about a company? My own experience with "cocoa beans" will give you a clue.

"Cocoa Beans"

While the vast majority of my portfolio is invested according to the strategies recommended in this book, I allocate a very small portion of my holdings to what I call my entertainment account. Several years ago, on the advice of a friend, I used a portion of my entertainment account to buy 30,000 shares of Coastal Caribbean, at a price of about 30 cents. This obscure company, which my friend affectionately calls "cocoa beans," trades on the equally obscure Boston Exchange, which is not listed in any local paper I know of. Wherever it finds the space, the *Wall Street Journal* inserts the Boston Exchange listings, but you really have to dig hard to find them.

With only two employees and no current or near-term revenue, the company has been losing money for over 40 years. To stay in business it occasionally issues additional shares in order to raise capital. Why did I invest in what seems to be an insolvent company? Coastal Caribbean's sole asset, and I use the term loosely, is a pending lawsuit against the state of Florida, in conjunction with drilling rights it owns to some of the most promising oil sites remaining in or near the United States. The only problem is that the sites are in very environmentally sensitive areas like the Everglades and Florida's coastal waters. As one of the shareholders, I hope the company receives a drilling permit. If it does, the financial rewards from owning this stock will be the equivalent of hitting a grand slam, with your team trailing by three runs, with two outs, in the bottom of the ninth, in the seventh game of the World Series.

While this case torturously makes its way through the courts, the stock hardly ever trades, and it is virtually impossible to learn anything new about the company.

"Nobody knows about it." *Right.* One day the friend who initially recommended the company to me left a message on my answering machine advising me that there was some good news on the company. However, before I could reach him, he left for the day. I called another friend, who also owns the stock, to tell him there might be some good news.

Not only did he have the news already, he proceeded to share the details with me, right off the Internet, regarding a favorable (though preliminary) ruling the company had received from the court. Of course, the stock was trading on very heavy volume. The price, which had gradually risen over the past few years, jumped instantaneously from about two to over three. There are no secrets. If there ever was a time when the markets were inefficient, that certainly is no longer the case.

The next time someone tells you that you should buy the stock of some company because he or she has information that has not yet been incorporated by the market into the price of the stock, remember the cocoa beans story. It's more than likely that the informant either is not correct about the market or has inside information. If it is the latter, remember that people can go to jail for trading on inside information.

Do Markets Value Stocks Correctly?

Some people have a problem with the efficient market concept when they see the price of a particular stock go from 30 one day to 20 the next. If the markets are so efficient, how can a company's worth vary by tens of millions of dollars from one day to the next? The problem stems from the question itself; it confuses the concept of market efficiency with the concept of current valuation. Defining a market as efficient, once again, means that the market incorporates everything that is known about a stock (including forecasts of future earnings, and so on) into its current valuation, or price.

Louis Bachelier, a French economist, long ago remarked: "Clearly the price considered most likely by the market is the true correct price: if the market judged otherwise it would not quote this price, but another price higher or lower."[46] Prices will not change if the expected happens. In an efficient market, any new information the market receives will be random, not in the sense of being good or bad, but in the sense of whether or not it surpasses or falls short of market expectations. The market quickly incorporates the new information and revalues the security. The volatility of both the stock and bond markets is evidence of the frequency with which the expected fails to occur.

How quickly the fixed income markets incorporate new information is amazing. Consider the following. Recent studies indicate that a considerable portion of the changes in interest rates can be attributed to scheduled macroeconomic announcements such as employment reports and inflation data. The major adjustment to the information release (and the window for trading profits) lasts about *40 seconds*.[47]

The speed of the stock market's response to new information is almost as startling. A recent study on the after-trading-hours quarterly earnings announcements of one hundred NYSE and one hundred NASDAQ firms found that the majority of the price response is realized during the *opening* trade. For earnings announcements that occurred during trading hours, the results were not much different. For NYSE stocks, the price adjustment occurred during the first several postannouncement trades. For NASDAQ stocks, the price adjustment was concentrated in the first postannouncement trade.[48] One can only conclude that the markets are very efficient at processing information and incorporating that information into valuations.

Let's look at an example. On the evening of January 23, 1997, Cascade Communications reported that its fourth quarter earnings had risen more than 100 percent from the previous quarter. The stock had closed the previous day at just over 64. "In a private off-the-record conversation Cascade's president indicated to a select group of Wall Street analysts that the next quarter would be flat—a devastating setback for a company whose share price was predicated on a vision of almost unending growth." Before the market could even open the next day, in after-hours trading on Instinet, Cascade dropped over 30 percent to $44.[49] Market efficiency is not about valuation; it is about how quickly market prices incorporate available information. It is about the effectiveness of active versus passive management.

Good News, Bad Results

On February 4, 1997, after the market had closed, Cisco Systems reported that its second quarter earnings had risen from $.31 per share in the prior year period to $.51, an increase of 65 percent. Certainly, no one would suggest that a rise in earnings of that magnitude is bad news. Yet the price of Cisco's stock fell the following day from its prior close of just over 67 to 63, a drop of

6 percent. The market's reaction can be explained by the efficient markets theory. Simply put, the market was anticipating a greater increase in earnings than the company reported. Prior to a company's release of information, outsiders do not know whether it will report earnings higher or lower than market expectations. In other words, whether subsequent information will affect the price of a stock in a positive or negative manner is random. The market incorporates new information and appropriately adjusts a stock's valuation.

Bad News, Good Results

A similar phenomenon occurs when a company's stock price rises after a "bad" earnings report. For example, the day IBM released its earnings for the second quarter of 1996, the price of its stock rose 13 percent. Based on the price movement, one would have thought that IBM had announced spectacular results. Their earnings were, in fact, down about 20 percent from the same period of the prior year. The stock rose because the market was expecting IBM to announce far worse results. The market's valuation was correct before the news release (based on everything that could then be known about the company) and was also correct after adjusting to the new information.

Active Management and Efficient Markets

While whether or not the market is efficient is an important question, because it has practical implications in determining the winning investment strategy, the only real question about which investors should be concerned is: Can anyone outsmart the market through active portfolio management? In commenting on active management, Paul Samuelson, one of our most well-known and respected economists (you probably used his textbook in Economics 101), wrote: "A respect for evidence compels me to the hypothesis that most portfolio managers should go out of business. Even if this advice to drop dead is good advice, it obviously will not be eagerly followed. Few people will commit suicide without a push."[50] Simply eloquent.

Timing the Market

I'm the lousiest market timer in the history of the market.
—Charles Clough, Chief Market Strategist, Merrill Lynch, quoted in the *Wall Street Journal,* October 29, 1997

My favorite time-frame is forever.   —Warren Buffett

Our stay-put behavior reflects our view that the stock market serves as a relocation center at which money is moved from the active to the passive.   —Warren Buffett

It has been a problem since the dawn of the retail brokerage business: Brokers have a strong incentive to get customers to trade when it might be in clients' interests to do nothing.
—*Business Week,* July 14, 1997

If portfolio managers cannot pick stocks, can they add value by trying to time their investment decisions (as opposed to a buy and hold strategy)? In order to believe in this approach, a manager must believe that he or she knows more—has better information—than the rest of the market; that the market is either under- or overvalued (i.e., the rest of the market is wrong). There is one simple piece of historical data I believe will convince even the most ardent of skeptics that trying to time investment decisions is an exercise in futility.

During the 3,541 trading days of 1980–1993, an investor who built and held a portfolio consisting of the S & P 500 would have realized annualized returns of 15.5 percent per annum. If, in an attempt to time the market, an investor missed out on just the best 10 days, the annualized return dropped to 11.9 percent. This investor, by being absent from less than 0.3 percent of the trading days, would have lost over 23 percent of the returns available for the entire period. If the same investor had had the misfortune of missing out on the best 40 days (or about 1 percent of the total trading days), his or her annualized returns would have dropped to 5.5 percent, a loss of almost two-thirds of the passive investor's returns. Another way of looking at this is that the returns of the investor who missed out on just the best 40 days could have been matched by owning risk-free certificates of deposit at a local bank.

Why Market Timing Doesn't Work: Annualized Returns for the S & P 500

1980–1993	Returns*
3,541 Trading Days	15.5%
Minus 10 best days	11.9
Minus 20 best days	9.5
Minus 30 best days	7.4
Minus 40 best days	5.5

*S & P 500 Index (price appreciation only; returns don't include dividends)
Source: Smith Barney Research Department

Trying to time investment decisions just doesn't work because most of the action occurs over such brief, and unexpected, periods of time. Despite that, there are "professional" Wall Street market timers who claim they can pick the best 1 percent of all trading days and who will spend much of their time, and your money, on this futile endeavor. "These professionals would do well to learn from deer hunters and fishermen who know the importance of 'being there' and using patient persistence—so they are there when opportunity knocks."[51]

A study of one hundred large pension funds and their experience with market timing found that while they all had engaged in at least some market timing, not one had improved its rate of return as a result. In fact, 89 of them lost as a result of their efforts, and their losses averaged an incredible 4.5 percent over a five-year period.[52]

Another study, covering the 10-year period 1984–1994, found that poor market timing cost mutual fund investors about 1 percent per year. The news was doubly disheartening because poor investment decisions and transaction costs left active fund managers with a total shortfall in performance of 2 percent per year or more.[53] Mutual fund cash flows repeatedly go to asset categories near their performance peaks and leave quickly after returns level off or fall. Unfortunately, the investment industry contributes to this result by heavily advertising funds with favorable short-term performance.

The following may be my favorite story on market timing. A Morningstar study evaluated 199 no-load growth mutual funds for which they had performance data for the period 1989–1994. The average total return for the 199 funds over this six-year period was 12.01 percent. The individual owners of those same funds (keeping in mind that the average no-load mutual fund investor holds his or her funds for only 21 months) for their various periods of ownership received a return, however, of just 2.02 percent. Either market timing or chasing the hot manager turned their 12 percent returns into 2 percent.[54] In a similar study it was found that investors in stock-owning mutual funds earned on average 10 percent less than the funds themselves in each of the 12 years from 1984 to 1996.[55]

There is another reason that trying to time investment decisions doesn't work. As we discussed earlier, the market moves in a random manner. The period 1926–1995 covers 840 months. If one corrects for the natural upward bias of the market, a mean monthly change of +0.6 percent, one ends up with 50.6 percent of the months positive and 49.4 percent negative. The first quartile observation is −2.78 percent, and the third quartile observation is +2.91 percent. Almost perfect symmetry. The random nature of the market is also revealed by the small number of runs in which the market moves in the same direction as in the preceding month. A movement in the same direction for two months in a row occurred only half the time; runs as long as five months occurred just 10 percent of the time.[56]

The day after the DJIA crossed the 6,000 mark, George Vanderheiden, who manages $28 billion at Fidelity Investments, stated, "The past few years are littered with the forecasts of people who have tried to time the market." Mr. Vanderheiden should know, because worries about corporate earnings growth made him go 15 percent into bonds in 1995, causing him to miss part of the market's gain.[57]

How Legends Are Made

One of my favorite films is *The Man Who Shot Liberty Valance*, a story about a greenhorn, pacifist lawyer (Jimmy Stewart) who stands up to and then shoots and kills the villain, Liberty Valance (Lee Marvin). When Stewart, now a U. S. senator, returns to his hometown to attend the funeral of his best friend (John Wayne), he relates the tale of the legendary gunfight in an interview with a young newspaper reporter. The reporter eventually learns that it was not Stewart but John Wayne who actually killed Liberty Valance; excited about his great discovery, he races off to his editor. When the editor finishes reading this incredible tale, he rips the reporter's notes to shreds and tells him: "When the legend becomes fact, print the legend."

In an attempt to generate business, investment firms also build legends; they go out of their way to create auras of greatness around their prognosticators, who, having made one or two accurate predictions, are promoted as experts capable of forecasting market movements. My college professor and mentor gave me this advice as I was about to embark on my career: "If you are going to forecast, forecast often; eventually you will get it right. And if you forecast a number, never give a date." And Winston Churchill said: "The greatest lesson in life is to know that even fools are right sometimes." Investors, of course, generally only hear about the "expert's" accurate forecasts. Investors almost never hear anything when the experts inevitably fall from grace. As investment advisor John Merrill says, "Strict and thorough accountability would ruin the game—so it is ignored."[58] The self-interested Wall Street establishment does, indeed, print the legend.

There is no better example of this than the rise and inevitable fall of a contemporary market guru, Elaine Garzarelli. While working at Shearson Lehman, Ms. Garzarelli was deemed a market guru when she correctly forecasted the 1987 crash based on a model that used a proprietary group of indicators that were thought to be able to predict market movements. Shearson Lehman began to widely tout her ability to call market moves; she also received considerable attention from the print and electronic media. Remember, the media creates gurus so that their audiences feel privileged to receive their insights. Ms. Garzarelli's forecasts even began to receive credit for moving the market itself. Eventually, Shearson Lehman rewarded her for her successful prognostications with a mutual fund of her own to manage. Let's look at her record.

By June 30, 1994, the fund she was managing, the Smith Barney/ Shearson Sector Analysis Fund, had risen in value by 38 percent over the five years she was in charge. During this same period the DJIA had risen in value by 74 percent. In other words, she managed to underperform that benchmark by about 50 percent. As Casey Stengel said, "You could look it up."

In May 1996, with the Dow surpassing 5,700, this well-known market guru, who had left Shearson Lehman to form her own firm, advised her clients to invest aggressively, since she foresaw the market heading for a new high of 6,300 by year end. Almost immediately, the market underwent a sharp correction, falling over 400 points. Perhaps Ms. Garzarelli's crystal ball began to cloud over, because at this point she reversed direction. Now she advised her clients to sell because her indicators called for a further large negative correction. Once again the market reversed course. By November the DJIA had crossed 6,500.

In November 1996, despite her misreadings of the market, Ms. Garzarelli touted her "successful track record" in a major direct mail promotional campaign. The mailing claimed that she had predicted every bear market in the past twenty years. The *Wall Street Journal* called it "one of the most alarming pieces of junk mail in Street history," and noted that "there has been only one crash in that time, but let's not get picky. If the market crashes any time in the next twenty years, the guru, or at least her public relations people, can say she had it right again."[59]

Continuing the saga, in January 1997, with the market approaching 7,000, Ms. Garzarelli reversed position once again and advised her clients to buy. By April the market had dropped to under 6,400.

Not yet convinced? For ten years the *Wall Street Journal*, with

assistance from two research firms, Wilshire Associates and Carpenter Analytical Services, studied the asset allocation advice
of strategists at the nation's largest brokerage houses, including
Lehman Brothers, Goldman Sachs, Paine Webber, Prudential,
Smith Barney, Merrill Lynch, and others. The *Journal* concluded
that "a decade of results throws cold water on the notion that
strategists exhibit any special ability to time the markets. The
average annual gain from their allocation decisions was a mere
.18 percent." This figure ignored the transaction costs and taxes
incurred as a result of the trading decisions. Once these were
taken into account, the value these strategists added would
clearly have been negative.[60]

There are temptations everywhere, especially tempting when
offered by notable market gurus. But remember that market
timers simply run too great a risk of being absent when the market makes one of its very infrequent but very large moves that are
the big determinants of performance. At the risk of being redun-
dant: If an investor had missed out on just the best 0.3 percent of
all trading days during the period 1980–1993, returns would have
been slashed by 23 percent. In the final analysis, market timing is
"much ado about nothing."

Market Timing Strategists and Weathermen

One of the most respected people on Wall Street is Barton
Biggs, Morgan Stanley's director of global strategy. Mr. Biggs
appeared on the cover of the July 19, 1993, issue of *Forbes* wearing a bear costume, warning investors: "Except for that nasty jolt
in October 1987, most investors under 40 have never experienced
a bear market. We have all been spoiled by 12 fat years." Convinced that the U. S. market had gotten way ahead of itself
(meaning that all other investors were wrong to have bid the mar-

ket up to such lofty levels), Biggs advised his clients to reduce
their exposure to the U. S. market to 18 percent of their portfolio
and to move their money overseas. He argued that the U. S. market was near its top and was due for a fall that could range from
20 percent to 50 percent. "If the S & P 500 Index registers one
of its average cyclical declines . . . it could have a precipitous
drop . . . to somewhere between 2800 and 2275. We are due for a
secular bear market . . . the decline could be 50 percent." He
added, "While the U. S. has had a tremendous bull market, the
European markets have been sluggish or worse. It doesn't take a
genius to see that this relationship is due for a change."

Over four years later, Mr. Biggs was still waiting for the bear
market that he was sure was overdue. During this period the
United States experienced its greatest bull market ever (one that
Mr. Biggs's clients presumably missed out on). In addition, despite his claim that "it doesn't take a genius to see that this relationship is due for to change," the U.S. market far outperformed
the European and emerging country markets—markets in which
Mr. Biggs was advising his clients to invest—by margins of
about two to one. If you can't trust Mr. Biggs or the venerable
Morgan Stanley, whom can you trust? In fact, Mr. Biggs himself
recently stated: "God made global strategists so that weathermen
would look good."[61] It seems he has a similar view to Warren
Buffett, who said, "The only value of stock forecasters is to make
fortune-tellers look good."[62]

Further Evidence on the Failure of Market Timing

Legendary investor Peter Lynch wondered whether market
timers really were able to avoid the inevitable corrections, or
whether in their efforts to do so they really only managed to
avoid the best months of the greatest bull markets. I think you

will agree with Lynch's conclusion that the answer is surely the latter. He points out that an investor who stayed fully invested in the S & P 500 over the 40-year period beginning in 1954 would have achieved an 11.4 percent rate of return. If that investor missed just the best 10 months (2 percent), the return dropped (27 percent) to 8.3 percent. If the investor missed the best 20 months (4 percent), the return dropped (54 percent) to 6.1 percent. Finally, if the investor missed the best 40 months (8 percent), the return dropped (76 percent) all the way to 2.7 percent. Do you really believe that there is anyone out there who can pick the best 40 months in a 40-year period?

Lynch tells an even more incredible story. If you had invested the same amount on January 1 of every year for 30 years beginning in 1965, your return would have been 11 percent per annum. If you had been unlucky enough to have invested the same dollar amount each year on the day that the S & P 500 Index hit its peak for that year, your return would still have been 10.6 percent per annum. That is less than a 0.5 percent per annum difference in returns. And no one is that unlucky. If, on the other hand, you were lucky enough to have chosen the market's low for the year, each year, then your return would have only increased to 11.7 percent per annum. That is an incremental return of just over 0.5 percent per annum. And no one is that lucky. If that does not qualify as much ado about nothing, I do not know what would.

Lynch concludes this tale by recalling that he has never once seen the name of a market timer on *Forbes*'s annual list of the richest people in the world. "If it were truly possible to predict corrections, you'd think somebody would have made billions by doing it."[63] Lynch got it almost right. While no individual has made billions from efforts to time the market, Wall Street firms that peddle this type of economic pandering certainly have made billions from the commissions on the trades of the individuals who listened to, and acted on, this type of fortunetelling.

Timing the market is a lot like playing slot machines. While it may be entertaining, the risk/reward trade-off is very poor. While we know that over the short term some slot machine players win, we neither attribute any skill to them nor expect them to win over the long term. The same is true of market timers. In the short term there will always be some who will make correct forecasts. Evidence has shown, however, that we should neither attribute any skill to the short-term winners nor expect them to beat the market in the future. The problem for investors is that market gurus who have made the most recent correct forecasts end up being interviewed by the financial press and the media. This attention somehow gives them an aura of credibility. It also, unfortunately, fuels the hopes of investors that there is a way to beat the market.

The body of evidence on the failure of efforts to time the market is so overwhelming that *Fortune* magazine recently reached this conclusion: "Let's say it clearly: No one knows where the market is going—experts or novices, soothsayers or astrologers. That's the simple truth."[64] This from the same magazine that advises you which active managers to choose when building your portfolio.

Whenever I am asked if it is a good time to invest, my advice is simple: The best time to invest is always whenever you have funds available to do so. Any other advice would simply be advising someone to play the loser's game. Remember that "the direction of the next 20 percent market move is both unknowable and immaterial to the success of a lifetime investment program. It's the direction of the next 100 percent move that matters, and we know perfectly well which way that'll be, now don't we?"[65] In other words, when the DJIA was at 4,000, no one knew whether the next move would be to 3,200 or to 4,800. However, everyone should have known that it would eventually hit 8,000 (which it did just four years later). Benjamin Disraeli said it best: "Patience is a necessary ingredient of genius."

Bubbles and Market Timing

It would certainly be useful if investors were able to determine when the market was too high (or too low) compared to its "value." Economists and investors have long attempted to determine whether bubbles exist. A bubble can be defined as what is left after market fundamentals have been removed from the price. Unfortunately, since neither bubbles nor market fundamentals are directly observable, one can never determine whether the market is too high given its fundamentals. We only know these things with hindsight. Harold Bierman, professor of business administration at Cornell, puts it this way: "There were people who predicted the 1929 crash and other people who predicted the 1987 crash. There might even be a few who predicted both. But, did they also predict other crashes between 1929 and 1987 that never happened? Were they also able to predict the market low and the right time to buy? Unfortunately, current economic theory does not provide us with the means to implement a market-timing strategy."[66]

There will always be a reasonable scenario that will justify the current level of the market. That's how it got there in the first place. Certainly, ex post facto, we can have a price bubble. Unfortunately, investors have no way of knowing if the price increase resulted from a bubble or from valid expectations. Only future events provide the answer. The best strategy: Ignore the experts and stay invested.

The Emperor Has No Clothes

The fairy tale of the Emperor's New Clothes provides an appropriate analogy to the belief in active management. In the children's fairy tale, a tailor convinces the emperor of the beauty of his nonexistent clothes. In the end, the emperor is embarrassed when he goes before the people believing in what is obviously not there. Just as the emperor was tricked by the tailor, investors are tricked by the investment community into believing in active management. The tailor relied on the emperor's ego; the emperor didn't want to admit that he couldn't see the tailor's miraculous cloth. Investors don't want to admit that neither they nor the investment managers they choose are capable of beating the market. They don't want to admit that they have been needlessly paying transaction costs and management fees. Charles Mackay, author of *Extraordinary Ordinary Popular Delusions and the Madness of Crowds*, said: "Every age has its peculiar folly: some scheme, project, or fantasy into which it plunges, spurred on by the love of gain, the necessity of excitement, or the force of imitation." He said this in 1841. It is just as true now as it was then.

Various academic studies provide evidence on the inability of professional investment managers to outperform the market. The most comprehensive study on mutual fund performance analyzed the performance of 1,892 funds for the period 1961–1993 and determined that the average equity fund underperformed the S & P 500 Index by about 1.8 percent per annum.[67] In an updated version of his own study, Mark Carhart found that expense ratios drive much of the persistent long-term underperformance of mutual funds; expenses were found to have at least a one-for-one negative impact on performance. He also found that turnover negatively impacts performance by 0.95 percent of the market value of the trade (reflecting transaction costs and spreads). Carhart's conclusion: "While the popular press will no doubt continue to glamorize the best-performing mutual fund managers, the mundane explanations of strategy (asset class allocation, not individual stock selection) and investment costs account for almost all of the important predictability in mutual fund returns."[68]

A recent Morningstar study found similar results—among actively managed U. S. diversified equity funds, high-turnover funds lag behind lower turnover funds for every time period studied (one, three, five, and ten years). And the higher the turnover, the worse the performance.[69]

Other studies have come up with similar results. Only 2 percent of portfolio returns are a result of market timing, and only 4 percent can be attributed to stock picking, while 94 percent can be accounted for by asset allocations.[70]

A study covering 143 mutual funds during the period 1965–1984 provides further support for the efficient markets theory. This study found that the average fund underperformed the S & P 500 Index by 1.59 percent per annum (notably, approximately the average fund's expense base). Even more striking, not a single fund produced a performance that was significantly positive from a statistical viewpoint.[71] It seems that the emperor really does have no clothes.

Active Managers' Response to Poor Performance: Enhanced Index Funds

Capitalism is a wonderful thing. Suppliers of product respond to demand. The popular press and media have finally begun to report on the poor performance of active managers. As more and more consumers become aware of their poor performance, as well as the risks that investing with them entails (more on this in a later chapter), mutual fund companies are rolling out new products. Some, in what I call a neither fish nor fowl mode, attempt to entice investors with a concept called "enhanced index funds." Such a fund, while basically trying to replicate an index such as the S & P 500, attempts to enhance returns (beat its index) by overweighting certain sectors of the market that it believes will perform better than the overall market. The managers of these enhanced index funds may also use complex options and futures contracts to make further "bets" on the direction of the market. In other words, while wearing sheep's clothing (a passive manager), there really is a wolf (an active manager) inside, charging higher fees for the so-called enhanced returns.

If you ever hear that the performance of index funds is disappointing, the creation of enhanced funds is one of the main culprits (although there are others). In trying to make it outperform its benchmark, the manager of the enhanced fund is engaging in the loser's game. Of the 11 enhanced index funds that use the S & P 500 Index as their benchmark, only three managed to beat the S & P 500 Index in 1995. The eight that failed to do so did so by an average of about 4 percent. Quite an achievement. I guess that begs the question, Exactly what does "enhanced" mean? Maybe it means enhanced profits for the fund managers in the form of the high fees they charge for the "enhanced" performance they fail to deliver.[72]

Charles Ellis points out another problem with enhanced index funds. He asks the questions: "How much do the actual portfolios differ from the index? What fees are investors paying *relative* to the assets composing this differentiated portfolio? The answers are daunting. If the typical enhanced index fund is even 20 percent differentiated from its index, then even a 0.5 percent apparent incremental fee is really a 2.5 percent marginal fee for the incremental differentiated portfolio."[73] If active managers have been unable to overcome their average expense base of 1.5 percent, how will they overcome a 2.5 percent handicap?

There are other reasons why index funds fail to match the performance of their benchmark. First, they incur expenses. These expenses include the cost of operating the fund, commissions on purchases and sales, and the profit margin the firm is seeking to achieve. Even if the assets within the fund exactly matched the assets that comprise the index, the fund would underperform its benchmark by an amount equal to its expenses. The greater the expense base, the greater the margin of underperformance. Some funds charge as little as 15 basis points (0.15 percent) per annum, while others may charge 50 or even 75 basis points (0.5 percent to 0.75 percent) per annum. These small differences may seem insignificant, but over long periods of time they can make a big difference in the total return of your portfolio.

> The index managers' dirty little secret is that while on the surface, all stock index funds should have identical returns, they don't because their expenses vary. Some index managers have admitted privately that high expenses exist because the funds feel they can get away with it. This is true because investors, thinking all index funds are the same, usually don't think to compare expenses. They think their expenses are all the same. For the one-year period ending March 27, 1997, the lowest cost S & P 500 Index fund produced returns of 22.3 percent as compared to the 21.5 percent return of the highest cost fund.[74]

A second reason index funds do not exactly match their benchmark is that in an attempt to reduce expenses, or increase their profit margin, many do not actually hold the same securities, in the same proportion, that comprise the index. Many funds try to match the performance of an index by selecting from the stocks that make up the index a smaller sample of stocks that have historically mirrored that index. They may choose just 50 percent of the stocks in the index (i.e., 250 out of the 500 that comprise the S & P 500 Index) and hope that past relationships continue to hold true. By owning just 50 percent of the stocks, they can reduce expenses. On the other hand, they are gambling that the past correlation between their sample and their benchmark will continue. This strategy leaves them open to either under- or outperforming their benchmark. Is that a bet you want to take?

If you decide to buy an index fund, the conclusions that I hope you have drawn are:

- Choose only index funds that are true index funds. Avoid those funds that try to replicate, but not duplicate, their benchmark index.

- Because index funds cannot add value (similar index funds should be buying and holding the same exact group of assets), you should choose the index fund with the lowest cost because it will provide you with the highest return.

- The term "enhanced index fund" is an oxymoron.

While a true index fund is likely to outperform active managers in the long run, I will show how you can achieve returns superior to these benchmarks by choosing passive asset class funds. There is an important distinction between index funds and passive asset class funds; for now, a definition will suffice. The difference between them is like the difference between a square and a rectangle. While all squares are rectangles, not all rectangles are squares. Likewise, while all index funds are passively managed (or at least they should be), not all passive asset class funds are index funds. The commonality is that they are both passive. Index funds attempt to replicate the performance of a popular benchmark index such as the S & P 500 or the Russell 2000. Passive asset class funds, on the other hand, attempt to replicate the performance of an asset class (a group of assets with similar risk characteristics), such as small-cap value stocks or emerging market stocks, for which no index may exist. I will revisit this important distinction later in greater detail.

Can Active Management Work in "Inefficient Markets"?

One final point on the efficiency of markets. Because of the overwhelming body of evidence, heretofore skeptical practitioners have started to concede that the market is efficient, at least with respect to the stocks of the companies with a large market capitalization; there are so many analysts following these companies that information about them is available to everyone and the competition is too tough. On the other hand, the same practitioners hold that the efficient market thesis is not true for the stocks of smaller companies, which are less widely followed and on which less information is available. In fact, the evidence for efficient markets is just as compelling for the smaller capitalization stocks as it is for the larger capitalization stocks. Statistics show that active managers in the asset class of small-cap companies perform no better than do active managers in the asset class of large-cap companies.

Emerging Markets

The same practitioners also cling to the belief that stock selection can add value in the underresearched and "inefficient" capital markets of the emerging industrial countries such as Mexico, Brazil, Singapore, or Turkey. If active management can produce superior results to a passive strategy, it should certainly be able to do so in these "inefficient" markets, where research can theoretically uncover undervalued securities.

First, let's deal with the myth that the financial markets of the emerging countries are underresearched. The Turkish Stock Exchange, for example, has about two hundred stocks and about 180 brokerage firms. It also has a modern, totally computerized trading system. It doesn't sound like the Turkish market lacks coverage for its securities or that its market is backward. However, if the financial markets of the emerging markets are truly inefficient, then we should find that active managers are beating the market averages. Once again, the evidence is to the contrary.

Dimensional Fund Advisors, a large institutional money manager, uses only a passive approach with its emerging markets fund. Although its three-year history covers a relatively brief period, the passively managed DFA fund dramatically outperformed the similar but actively managed funds of Merrill Lynch, Templeton, Fidelity, Morgan Stanley, and many other similar well-known funds—which leads me to ask the question: If you cannot beat the "inefficient markets," how can you beat the efficient markets? (See Exhibit B.)

Micropal, a London-based research firm, found similar results when they looked at Global, Asian, and Latin American emerging market funds, for the three-year period ending June 30, 1996, and compared their performance to the Barings Index for those sectors.

EFFICIENT MARKETS AND MODERN PORTFOLIO THEORY

Micropal Emerging Market Indices	Number of Funds	Three-Year Sector Average Total Return	Barings Index
Global	95	+24.68%	+39.70%
Asia	169	+34.41%	+58.35%
Latin America	53	+22.21%	+31.71%

Source: Micropal

In not one case did the active managers come close to matching the performance of their benchmark indices.

The Efficiency of International Markets

Thanks to David Booth of DFA, we now have further empirical evidence against the often-heard argument that because international markets are not as well researched and therefore not as efficient as the U. S. markets, active managers can add value when investing globally.

Booth compared the performance of single country funds to an appropriate benchmark, a country index. His study covered nine countries and 26 funds in developed markets, and 18 countries and 30 funds in emerging markets. If active managers are able to add value, one would see them consistently outperforming market indices. All results are for the period ending December 1996. Booth found that while the average developed market country fund outperformed its benchmark by 0.7 percent over a one-year period, it managed to underperform by 7.9 percent and 1.4 percent over three- and five-year periods, respectively. The average emerging market country fund also underperformed its benchmark country index by 11.8 percent, 5.8 percent, and 1.6 percent over one-, three-, and five-year periods, respectively. The average underperformance for all 56 funds covering 27 countries was 7.9

percent, 6.6 percent, and 1.5 percent for one, three, and five-year periods, respectively. The value added by active managers is clearly negative. In addition, the negative value added is greatest in the emerging markets, the very markets where active managers claim to add the most value (because they believe these markets to be the most inefficient).

The main reason for this result is that the costs of trading in the less efficient overseas markets are greater than in the more efficient U. S. markets—and the more inefficient the market, the greater the trading costs. Again one sees that despite the claims of active managers, there is no evidence that active management works in either efficient or inefficient markets. Booth concluded: "Even these dismal results overstate the value of active managers since the benchmark indices are price-only indices, rather than total return indices, which would include dividends." Even Booth's insight on total returns is not the whole story. For taxable accounts, the value added by active managers is likely to be even more negative due to the greater turnover, and probable greater distributed income of an active versus a passive management strategy.[75]

The Bottom Line

Since over 80 percent of all equity trading is carried out by institutions, through their skilled knowledgeable traders, it is very difficult to secure an advantage over the competition. I do not claim that it is impossible to beat the market. In fact, as I have shown, about 25 percent of active managers do so every year. However, as was so aptly put by active manager Robert Stovall, "It's a different group of them every year." Moreover, academic studies have demonstrated that the longer the time frame, the more the number of active managers who succeed at this loser's game decreases.

Perhaps the most impressive piece of data on the inability of active management to beat the market (thereby strengthening the argument that the markets are efficient) is contained in the chart that follows. It shows an incredibly high correlation between the ability of active managers to beat the market and the outcome of a coin-flipping contest.

Security Selection: Do active managers perform better than a random flipping of coins?

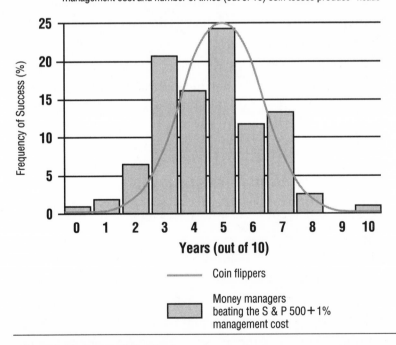

Number of years (out of 10) active money managers beat the S & P 500 +1% management cost and number of times (out of 10) coin tosses produce "heads"

Source: SEI investments (1984–1993)
Manager returns are calculated without subtracting fees.

If you put enough people together, some will flip 10 heads in a row. Similarly, if you have thousands of active managers, some will beat the market, possibly even 10 years in a row. Attributing a particular level of skill to the managers who beat the market, however, is the equivalent of attributing a particular skill to the winner of the coin-flipping contest. Put another way, believing that the winner of the coin-flipping contest will repeat his or her performance is comparable to believing that an active manager who beats his or her benchmark in one period will do so in the next period. If the markets were truly inefficient, one would observe far more successful money managers than just the handful of Peter Lynches and Warren Buffetts.

Efficient Markets and Bond Funds

Basically, we were guessing on interest rates . . . What we've come to believe is that no one can guess interest rates.
—Fred Henning, head of fixed income investing at
Fidelity Investments, *Los Angeles Times,* July 7, 1997

Although this book concentrates on the equity markets, it is important to at least touch on the fixed income portion of a portfolio. As with equity markets, if fixed income markets are not efficient, then one should observe active managers outperforming their benchmarks. If, on the other hand, the markets are efficient, then active managers will be playing a loser's game and will fail to outperform their benchmarks.

A study covering as many as 361 bond funds showed that the average actively managed bond fund underperforms its index by 85 basis points a year. Furthermore, depending on the benchmark, between 65 and 80 percent of the funds generated excess returns (returns from their active trading) that were negative.[76]

A 1994 study found that only 128 (16 percent) out of eight hundred fixed income funds beat their relevant benchmark over the 10-year period covered.[77]

John Bogle of Vanguard studied the performance of bond funds and concluded: "Although past absolute returns of bond funds are a flawed predictor of future returns, there is a fairly easy way to predict future relative returns." After he separated the bond funds into their major categories of quality and maturity, he analyzed returns in terms of their expense ratios. Bogle placed funds into four categories: those with expenses of less than 0.5 percent; those with expenses between 0.5 percent and 1 percent; those with expenses between 1 percent and 1.5 percent; and those with expenses of over 1.5 percent. He found that "In every case, and in every category, the superior funds could have been systemically identified based solely on their lower expense ratios. At the extremes, the lower expense funds outpaced the higher expense funds by between 1 percent and 2.2 percent annually. The ability to predict interest rates played no part in the performance of the bond funds."[78] The lesson for investors: If you want to invest in a bond fund, choose the fund that has the lowest expense ratio from among those funds that meet your credit quality and maturity requirements. Part 3 will provide you with the skills needed to accomplish this objective.

If you still think that professional economists can do a good job of forecasting interest rates, consider the results of this survey. On January 3, 1995, the *Wall Street Journal* asked 59 of the nation's top economists to forecast the 30-year treasury bond yield on December 31, 1995. The rate at year end 1994 was 7.87 percent. Gail Fosler of the prestigious Conference Board forecast the highest rate—8.75 percent—while Susan Sterne of Economic Analysis forecast the lowest—6 percent. The average forecast was 7.61 percent. Thirteen economists projected a rate over 8 percent, while only three projected a rate under 7 percent. The year actually ended with the 30-year treasury rate at 5.94 percent, putting the average margin of error at 1.67 percent. Of these economists, 95 percent had an average margin of error over 1 percent. One of the least accurate forecasts, at 8.4 percent, was made by a former Wall Street economist who had previously served as governor of the Federal Reserve.

A fitting conclusion to this story arrived when the *Wall Street Journal* published the results of their survey for the following year. The previous winner, Susan Sterne, had the least accurate prediction for 1996. She had predicted that the bond yield would finish at 5 percent versus the actual 6.64 percent.

Not yet convinced? Here is one more anecdote. The *Wall Street Journal* of January 2, 1997, reviewed the forecasts of its previous forecasting contest and deemed A. Gary Shilling the winner for the latest six-month period. Since his forecast for the 30-year treasury bond on December 31, 1995, was the most inaccurate, the *Journal* was prepared to give him an award as the comeback economist. His reaction: "Hollywood producers with all their market research dollars get paid zillions of dollars and they don't get it right. Why should I, a mere economist, do any better?"

The *Journal*'s survey provided further evidence on the efficiency of the markets. A recent study, based on the *Journal*'s survey since its inception in December 1981, found the following astonishing results.

- For the 36 forecast periods (it's a biannual survey), three-month treasury bill rates moved in the opposite direction of the consensus forecast 53 percent of the time. That was the

91

good news. For the 30-year bond the consensus was in the wrong direction 67 percent of the time.

- The average error of the three-month bill and 30-year bond forecasts was 79 and 86 basis points, respectively. If you had just assumed that rates would have remained unchanged, your forecast errors would have been 74 and 78 basis points, respectively.

- The more rates moved, the worse the forecast got. Of the 10 times that rates on the 30-year bond moved over one hundred basis points, the consensus forecast was in the wrong direction eight times. On one of the two times the consensus was in the right direction, it called for rates to fall just 18 basis points; the rate on the 30-year bond actually fell 102 basis points. Essentially, economists had missed 9 of the 10 largest moves in the past 16 years.

- Of the 44 economists who participated in at least 10 contests, only 13 (30 percent) guessed the direction right more than 50 percent of the time, and none were accurate more than 60 percent of the time.[79]

If the nation's top economists have such great difficulty forecasting interest rates, it seems illogical to expect that investment strategies based on interest rate forecasts can succeed.

Economists and active bond portfolio managers can do no better a job predicting interest rates than active equity managers can predicting stock prices. Active management of fixed income portfolios is just as much a loser's game as active management of equity portfolios.

To play the winner's game for fixed income portfolios, purchase passively managed fixed-income funds that do not spend your dollars in a futile attempt to beat the market by changing the maturity of their portfolio (lengthening maturities when they believe rates will fall and shortening them when they believe rates will rise) based on their forecasts of interest rates.

Efficient Markets and Costs

Beware of false prophets, which come in sheep's clothing, but inwardly are ravaging wolves. —Matthew 7:15

While the question of whether or not the market is efficient from an information perspective has important implications, it is not the only criterion one needs to consider in order to develop the appropriate investment strategy. I showed earlier in this chapter that the efficiency of the market in processing information makes active management a loser's game. Another factor that makes it a loser's game is that any advantage gained by exploiting alleged market inefficiencies may not be great enough to overcome the trading, research, and other costs incurred. As I will show, the costs incurred when entering into transactions play a very important role in determining the winning investment strategy. In this case market inefficiency, in terms of the costs of trading, helps make active management a loser's game.

The Bid-Offer Spread

A market can be said to be efficient when the cost to enter into a transaction is relatively low. Since managers incur the cost of the difference between the bid and offer prices when they trade, the bid-offer spread is a reasonably good estimate of the trading costs of a mutual fund. The average spread between the bid (the price at which people are willing to buy) and the offer (the price at which people are willing to sell) for the stocks of the first decile (the top 10 percent) of companies, ranked by market capitalization (size), is only 0.53 percent (see table). The average spread for the tenth decile (the bottom 10 percent) of companies is 6.19 percent.

The Smaller the Market Capitalization, the Higher the Potential Trading Costs and the Smaller the Daily Trading Volume

Size Decile	Average Price	Percent Spread	Daily Trading Per Issue	
			Shares	Dollars
1	53.92	0.53	904,445	47,294,212
2	42.70	0.60	506,539	19,300,213
3	38.19	0.71	336,778	10,772,236
4	33.12	0.98	211,360	5,354,680
5	27.32	1.25	164,897	3,697,177
6	25.79	1.26	117,658	2,645,244
7	22.87	1.61	88,745	1,636,101
8	19.16	2.21	60,099	846,424
9	14.84	2.99	37,894	415,914
10	8.35	6.19	17,462	119,259

We can conclude that the market for the largest-cap stocks is about 12 times as efficient as that for the smallest-cap stocks.

The reason this difference exists is that for the stocks in the first decile, daily trading volume averages almost one million shares, as opposed to less than 20 thousand shares for the stocks in the tenth decile. The difference is even more dramatic when one looks at dollar trading volume. For the first decile stocks, dollar volume averages almost $50 million, compared to a little over $100,000 for the tenth decile stocks. For the first decile stocks the greater number of buyers and sellers competing with each other leads to a very tight bid-offer spread and low trading costs. The wider spreads and greater costs in the tenth decile stocks is a direct result of the absence of this level of competition.

Markets characterized by large numbers of buyers and sellers, and the resulting small spreads, are called liquid or efficient markets. Markets with fewer buyers and sellers are less liquid and therefore less efficient. It is logical that the greater the number of buyers and sellers, the tighter will be the spreads and the lower the trading costs. The lower level of liquidity available in the small-cap sector makes trading in this asset class riskier than trading in the more liquid asset class of large-cap stocks. In the next chapter, I will show that the markets are efficient in pricing for risk. In other words, if an asset class is riskier, investors must be compensated with higher returns for accepting that higher level of risk.

Turnover

Let's now examine just how great an impact the bid-offer spread can have on the performance of active managers in their search for securities that the rest of the market has somehow mispriced. The average mutual fund has a turnover rate of about 80 percent. While turnover is best defined in dollar terms, it can also be thought of in the following way. If a fund held the stocks of one hundred companies at the beginning of the year, by the end of the year the buying and selling of stocks by the fund manager would result in the stocks of 80 of them being replaced by the stocks of 80 new companies. This means the fund must bear the expenses of selling 80 stocks and buying 80 new ones. One can approximate the cost of active management by multiplying the turnover rate by the bid-offer spread. For the first decile of stocks, the cost is 0.8 (80 percent) times approximately 0.5 percent (the bid-offer spread), or 4 percent. For the tenth decile stocks, the cost is 0.8 times approximately 6 percent, or 4.8 percent.

Passively managed funds, by definition, have very low turnover rates in comparison to actively managed funds. A passively managed small company fund might have a turnover of 15 percent per annum. With this knowledge, one can compare the trading cost hurdle (for the asset class of small-cap stocks) that active management imposes on itself to that of a passive strategy.

	Active Management	Passive Management
Turnover rate (a)	80.0%	15.0%
Bid–offer spread (b)	6.0%	6.0%
Trading costs (a × b)	4.8%	0.9%

The trading costs of active management create a significant hurdle of 3.9 percent per annum (4.8–0.9 percent), which must be overcome in order to match the performance of passive managers. As just shown, an actively managed small company fund (the ninth and tenth decile stocks) has to overcome the 4.8 percent hurdle created by its trading activity just to match its benchmark. And this figure excludes trading commissions. In reality, the impact of the turnover of active managers is greater than just illustrated, because the example ignores the market impact of the trading activity of active managers. If an active manager attempts to buy (or sell) in excess of the daily trading volume, the result will probably be that his or her actions will drive up (or down) the price. Given that they have such great hurdles to overcome, one might say that it is to the credit of the managers of actively managed small company funds that their performance is not worse than it actually is. The only problem is that since they are still delivering results below those delivered by passively managed funds, they would be better off not trying in the first place. So would their investors. That is why it is the loser's game.

As you can see, the more illiquid the market (the larger the bid-offer spread) the greater the hurdle an active manager has to overcome in order to add value. One can only imagine how much wider the spreads must be, and higher the transaction costs, when trading in the emerging markets of Brazil, Mexico, and so on. These wide spreads and high transaction costs go a long way toward explaining the poor performance shown here of actively managed emerging market funds as compared to their passively managed counterparts.

Costs Create Hurdles

The burden of overcoming the costs of active management is a major reason why active management doesn't work, even if the markets are, as many claim, relatively inefficient from a classical economic (i.e., information) perspective. While whether the markets are efficient from an information perspective is a very important ingredient in both understanding how markets work and in determining whether active or passive management will be the winning strategy, the whole debate about whether or not the markets are "efficient" is really somewhat irrelevant to the investment policy process. What really matters to investors is whether or not active management can overcome its expenses and add value over a passive strategy. A recent Morningstar study supports this view. Over the 10-year period studied, Morningstar found that low turnover funds (those with an average holding period greater than five years—or less than a 20 percent turnover rate) rose an average of 12.87 percent per annum, while high turnover funds (those with an average holding period of less than one year—or a turnover rate of greater than 100 percent) gained only 11.29 percent per annum on average. Trading costs and the impact on prices of trading activity reduced returns of the high turnover funds by 1.58 percent per annum.[80] As I have shown, the more illiquid the market, the more difficult it will be for active managers to succeed in their objective. To summarize, active management doesn't work well in efficient markets, and it doesn't work well in inefficient markets. It doesn't work well, period. It is the loser's game.

Explaining the Performance of the Superstars

The question I am most often asked is: "If the markets are so efficient, how do you account for the performance of such superstars as Peter Lynch and Warren Buffett?" The answer lies in the chart of coinflippers we explored earlier. We only know that Mr. Lynch and Mr. Buffett are the superstars of the investment world after the fact. With many thousands of investment managers trying to beat the market, we know that inevitably some will succeed. I have also shown that because of the many hurdles that these managers face in their efforts to beat the market, far fewer succeed than would randomly be expected to do so. The surprise, therefore, is not that a few managers did beat the market, but rather that so few succeeded in doing so. While one fully expects some to succeed, the problem is that it is impossible to know ahead of time which will be the lucky few. In other words, 20 years from now we will be talking about a few superstar investment managers who are the successors to Lynch and Buffett, but there is no way to predict who they will be.

Fortunately, you do not need the next Michael Jordan of investment managers to have a positive investment experience. The gains are, literally, there for the taking. As I will show, the key to success is gaining exposure to the right asset classes, diversifying your risk, and having the discipline to stick with the strategy.

Technical Analysis

If fifty million people say a foolish a thing, it is still a foolish thing. —Anatole France

As I have shown, active managers have had little success adding value through superior research. Before turning to the discussion in the next chapter on risk, let's take a look at one other strategy some active managers believe they can use to beat the market: technical analysis.

Millions of people believe in astrology. They believe that astrologists, by interpreting the alignment, or charts, of the planets and stars can predict the future. Astrologists make forecasts such as the following: "Bill Meridian, writing in the *Mountain Valley Astrologer*, believes that the bear will likely visit the stock market as Jupiter soon completes the most bullish part of its 12-year passage from Virgo through Sagittarius. Don't be downhearted, though. Jupiter moving into conjunction with Uranus in mid-February will touch off one of those bursts of technological creativity that accompany this planetary alignment in 14-year cycles."[81]

Millions of people also believe in technical analysis. They believe that technical analysts can predict future stock price movements by interpreting charts of past prices. Unfortunately for investors, technical analysis has no more basis in reality than astrology.

Technical analysts are a unique group. Like proponents of the efficient markets theory, they believe that fundamental security analysis, which focuses on predicting the performance of stocks based on predicted future earnings, is a futile endeavor. On the other hand, the efficient market theory states that no trading system can generate returns in excess of the market's return. Technical analysts believe, however, that they can identify mispriced assets based on historical price movements.

Technical analysts look at charts of historical prices to find patterns they believe will enable them to identify which direction, and by how much, prices will move in the immediate future. People engaged in this "art" used to be called chartists. In order to give them an air of authority and respectability they are now called technicians. If this style of analysis worked, one would be able to see managers who use this style of analysis beating the market. As already shown, no such evidence exists. While this lack of evidence should be sufficient to convince you, there is one dramatic story I believe will convince anyone, except those trying to sell you their technical analysis services.

In 1959, Harry Roberts of the University of Chicago had a computer generate a series of random numbers. He stipulated that it do so with a distribution that would match the average weekly price change of the average stock (about 2 percent). Since the numbers were randomly generated, there was no pattern and therefore no knowledge that could be obtained by studying a chart of this nature. In order to create the illusion that his charts were those of particular stocks, Roberts placed a starting price of $40 on each chart. He then took a group of these charts to the leading technical analysts of his day. He asked for their advice on whether to buy or sell these unnamed hypothetical stocks. He told them that he did not want them to know the name of the stock, since this knowledge might bias them. Each technical analyst had very strong advice on what Roberts should do; but since the numbers were randomly generated, the patterns were only in the minds of the observers. I am sure that you will never hear about this story from a technical analyst.

Despite the fact that the results of this study were published in the *Journal of Finance* in 1959, certainly embarrassing the technical analysis "profession," you can still observe technical analysts dispensing advice on CNBC, and investors are presumably acting on that advice.[82] In actuality, the only thing their advice is good for is entertainment. Taken any other way, it is dangerous to the financial health of the listeners, because it causes them to veer from the academically proven buy and hold strategy. As a test, see if you can pick out the randomly generated chart from the actual chart of weekly stock prices for 1956. The charts are replicas of ones that appeared in the aforementioned *Journal of Finance* article. Be sure to cover up the legend at the bottom.

Simulated or Actual?

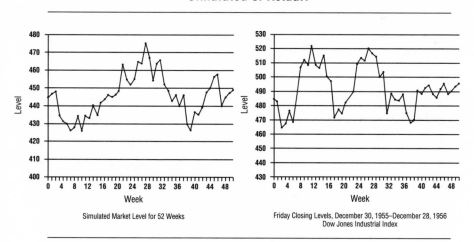

Simulated Market Level for 52 Weeks

Friday Closing Levels, December 30, 1955–December 28, 1956
Dow Jones Industrial Index

Source: Harry V. Roberts (University of Chicago), "Stock-Market 'Patterns' and Financial Analysis: Methodological Suggestions," *Journal of Finance 14: 1, March 1959.*

It is worth noting that Roberts's experiment has been repeated using the results of a computer-generated coin toss game. As you can see in the following chart, the computer will produce a randomly generated chart that moves around the expected 50 percent heads and 50 percent tails. It does look suspiciously like the chart of a stock's price movement. This is, by the way, further support of the efficient markets theory. As I explained earlier, stock prices do move in a random fashion as they respond to new information, which is random in whether it will be better or worse than the

Effects of Random Wandering on Coin-tossing Game
$1 Gain or Loss per Toss
Expected Return: $0.00

Number of Tosses	Average Return per Toss		95% Confidence Limits (+/−) Total Gain or Loss
	Low	High	
100	−20 to	20	+/−$20
10,000	−2 to	2	+/−$200
1 million	−0.2 to	0.2	+/−$2,000
100 million	−0.02 to	0.02	+/−$20,000
10 billion	−0.002 to	0.002	+/−$200,000

markets have anticipated. Technical analysts, if shown this chart, will give you a strong opinion on the future direction of the "stock" the chart is supposedly representing. (And George Bush thought that Ronald Reagan was practicing "voodoo economics.")

What I hope you have learned from this story is that while a picture (or chart) may be worth a thousand words, it is not worth even one of your investment dollars.

The following story is one of my favorite examples of the gibberish of technical analysis. The November 16, 1992, edition of *USA Today* carried the following forecast in Dan Dorfman's column. Being in Mr. Dorfman's column, of course, gave it immediate credibility. "Technical analyst Jerry Favors sees the DJIA plunging 400 points in the next few weeks, and dropping from 3,233 to 1,700 or less between May and June of 1993. The forecast is based on a 'three-peaks-and-a-dome-house' technical indicator he claims has never been wrong in the 25 or so times it has been activated in the last 200 years." Mr. Dorfman presumably carried this story because he thought that Mr. Favors was providing real value added for his clients. Mr. Dorfman also presumably thought his readers might want to consider acting on this advice (otherwise, why print the story?). Five years and over 4,000 points later, investors who sold their investments based on Mr. Favors's forecast were still waiting for the correction that was predicted. If you are not yet convinced that three-peaks-and-a-dome and an indicator that never failed in over two hundred years isn't gibberish and investment pandering, I certainly am not accomplishing my mission. I hope that you have learned that even if such a thing ever existed, it was just another example of a random pattern with no predictive value.

As Burton Malkiel points out: "If you examine past stock prices in any given period, you will always find some kind of system that would have worked in a given period. If enough different criteria for selecting stocks are tried, one will eventually be found that selects the best ones for that period." Malkiel cites a study in which a computer was programmed to draw charts for 548 stocks traded on the New York Stock Exchange (NYSE) over a five-year period. It was instructed to scan all the charts and identify any one of 32 of the most popularly followed patterns. Whenever the computer identified a bearish or bullish chart pattern, it recorded the appropriate sell or buy signal. The conclusion of the study was that there was no relationship between technical signals and subsequent performance. After brokerage expenses, the performance of the technical indicators was no better than a buy and hold strategy. In fact, the strategy that came closest to producing above-average results was to buy after one of the bear signals.[83]

If technical analysis has no basis in reality, why do many Wall Street firms hire people to perform this particular brand of fortune-telling? My guess: it is just another form of the greater fool theory. Wall Street firms hope to persuade investors to generate greater trading activity and therefore more commission income. Unfortunately, the media contribute to the appearance that technical analysts add value by giving them space in print and time on the air. CNBC even has its own technical analysis guru. You may want to listen for the entertainment value; I personally find the gibberish that they spout occasionally amusing, even when at times their advice is unintelligible. But remember that they are as useful as the astrological forecast discussed earlier in this chapter.

One of the best pieces of advice I can give you is that when a technical analyst appears on your television, do what I usually do when a commercial comes on—hit the mute button.

CHAPTER 4

◆

Efficient
Markets II—Risk

Though this be madness, yet there is method in't.
—Shakespeare, *Hamlet,* act 2, scene 2

The third category of market efficiency, and probably the most important factor to be used in developing the winning investment strategy, is risk. Fortunately, this concept is the easiest to grasp. It can really be all summed up in the cliché "Nothing ventured, nothing gained." It is important to understand that markets are efficient, meaning rational, in how they price for risk. If markets are efficient, then assets that are riskier will provide higher returns as compensation for their greater risk. If less risky assets produced higher returns, you would have what economists call a free lunch.

Imagine a world in which you could buy a U. S. government security carrying a higher yield than a corporate bond with a similar maturity; this world would not make any sense. The government security carries no credit risk. The corporate bond carries with it some degree of default risk. Being riskier, the corporate bond must provide a higher yield to attract investors. However, if such an anomaly existed, investors would immediately sell corporate bonds, driving their price down (and yield up), and buy government bonds, driving their price up (and yield down), until the anomaly no longer existed. Their actions would drive the price differential between the two securities to the level at which investors were exactly compensated for the perceived difference in risk. This process, by the way, is called arbitrage. I will now examine how an investor can utilize this knowledge about the relationship between risk and return to develop his or her own winning strategy.

Returns and Cost of Capital

We know that corporations must pay a higher rate of interest (they have a higher cost of capital) than the U. S. government. We also know that corporations with low credit ratings must pay more (have a higher cost of capital) than corporations with high credit ratings. We know, too, that the flip side of a high cost of capital is a high return to those who provide that capital (a very important piece of knowledge). Why, then, shouldn't an investor in search of high returns buy the bond of just one company with a low credit, that is, junk bond rating? The answer is that the investor might be unlucky enough to buy the bond of a company that will eventually go bankrupt. In order to insure that the investor receives the rate of return that the market requires the group of companies with the same risk characteristics (or asset class) to pay for its capital, the investor needs to, in effect, buy the bonds of all the companies within that risk category (or asset class). This is what is meant by diversifying your risk. To use another cliché, "Don't put all your eggs in one basket." The same diversification strategy can be applied to equity investments.

Returns and Risk

Over the last 70 years, cash equivalents, such as treasury bills and bank certificates of deposit, have produced less than a 1 percent rate of return, after inflation is taken into account. U. S. treasury bonds, which entail no credit risk, but do carry interest rate risk (if rates rise, they will fall in value), provided an after-inflation (or real) rate of return of a little more than 2 percent. The S & P 500 Index (a proxy for an investment in the stock market) provided far superior returns; it increased at an after-inflation rate of about 6 percent.

By the way, I have just shown that the markets are efficient. The riskier the asset, the greater the return to investors. It is worth noting that a 6 percent real per annum rate of return results in a real (in terms of purchasing power) doubling of your original investment over approximately every 12-year period. This is why I like to say that while savers (those who save in the form of cash or bonds) may sleep well, investors (those who invest, or risk, their savings in equity investments) eat well.

Savings Versus Investments

This differentiation between savings and investments is a very important concept to understand. Savings, because of their low risk, and therefore low return, should be accumulated to meet emergency needs, income needs, and short-term (less than 3–10 years) spending requirements, such as college tuition. Once you have created this safety net, the balance of your capital should be invested. This combination of savings and investments (your portfolio's asset allocation) will enable you to ride out the often dramatic fluctuations in the market because you have confidence in the long-range success of your investment strategy.

There is no one right portfolio for everyone. Each individual's needs for savings are different. Everyone's investment time horizons are also different. In addition, not everyone can have peace of mind and accept the inevitable bad years. One purpose of this book is to give you the information necessary to empower you to make your own asset allocation decisions.

Equities Produce the Highest Returns

As just shown, equities historically have produced much higher returns than either short- or long-term fixed income investments. In order to be confident that they will continue to provide superior returns, we need to question whether this superior performance was logical. We need to ask the question: Why do equities produce greater returns? The answer is simple: They must, or investors wouldn't accept the greater risk that they entail compared to bonds. Taking it one step further, companies that the markets perceive as riskier have a higher cost of capital. In other words, riskier companies have to give away more of their expected future earnings in order to raise capital than do their safer counterparts. Investors demand these greater returns as the compensation for taking greater risk.

This is very powerful knowledge. If we can now just identify the asset classes with the highest returns, and buy and hold all the securities within those asset classes (since we already know that the odds are stacked against investors attempting to pick individual securities or time investment decisions), we can earn returns in excess of the market's average return, a feat that few professional investors have accomplished, as we have already learned. By building a broadly diversified global portfolio of high-risk (and therefore high-return) securities for the portion of our portfolio allocated to equities, we eliminate the risk associated with investing in just one security, one industry, or even one country. It would be impractical for an individual investor to build such a portfolio without using passively managed asset class mutual funds.

Finding High-Return Asset Classes

The more original a discovery, the more obvious it seems afterward.   —Arthur Koestler

Identifying the highest yielding asset classes is actually a lot easier than you might have thought. Since it is known that risk is associated with return, all one has to do is identify the riskiest asset classes. One starts by comparing the asset classes of stocks and bonds. Since it is known that because stocks are riskier than bonds they must provide greater returns—as in fact they have for every single 15-year period over the past 70 years—one now turns to trying to identify the highest cost of capital equity asset classes. The answer is intuitive. Companies that have the highest cost of capital are risky small companies and risky "lousy" (or "value") companies.

"Lousy" or distressed companies are those trading closest to their liquidation value. One can identify these companies by their book value-to-market value ratio. "Book value" is a term for a firm's net worth (assets minus liabilities) from an accounting perspective. The higher the book-to-market value ratio, the closer a company is to being worth more dead than alive. The use of this book-to-market value definition is why these companies are called value stocks. Investors, through their market trading activities, have driven down the prices of value companies because these companies have produced poor track records. Therefore, they are perceived to be risky.

Small companies are also generally perceived as risky because they do not have the deep pockets to survive a prolonged period of financial turmoil. (Chrysler, a large company, may or may not be perceived as a great company, but it has a large cash reserve that it could use to carry it through a prolonged recession.) Small companies also do not, as a rule, have long proven track records of success. Lousy or value companies, in contrast, have proven track records, only they are currently poor ones.

Robert Merton, a prominent financial economist at Harvard, provides further explanations of why small companies are riskier, have higher costs of capital, and therefore provide higher returns. He postulates that the neglect of analysts and institutions results in a lack of information—increasing the risks to investors, and therefore the cost of capital to the firm. This hypothesis has been confirmed by studies focusing on investor relations. He also states that a key determinant of the size of the spread quoted by market makers (a proxy for the cost of trading) is information asymmetry facing the market maker. In other words, when market makers believe that some investors have superior knowledge, the bid–offer spread widens (increasing the cost of active management) as a form of protection.[84]

Think of risk and the market in these terms: Microsoft is now a much larger company and a lot less risky investment than it was 10 years ago. It also has many more analysts following the company. If it were to raise capital today, it would pay a lot less for that capital than it did when its stock first went public. Since it is a safer investment today, investors should expect to receive a lower future return.

Citicorp is a safer investment today than it was just a few years ago when some thought its credit losses might even bring it down. Today, because it has returned to profitability and restored its capital base, its cost of equity capital is lower than it paid to investors just a few short years ago (when it was a value company). Therefore, investors who purchase Citicorp's stock today can expect to earn a lower return than did investors in the recent past. Returns are compensation for risk.

The fact that investments in the stocks of both Microsoft and Citicorp are likely to produce lower expected returns than they did when they were small and value companies, respectively, does not make them bad investments. It does mean, however, that investors seeking a lower risk profile should expect lower returns. Investors must decide for themselves whether they want higher returns, and will accept the risk that goes along with those higher expected returns, or whether they want a lower level of risk, and are willing to accept the lower returns associated with that reduced level of risk.

I have just shown that risky companies make great investments. However, if you are not yet convinced that great companies don't make great investments, here is one story I believe will convert you.

Great Companies Do Not Make Great Investments

Let us take you back in time to 1964. John Doe is the best security analyst in the world. He is able to identify, with uncanny accuracy, the companies that will perform the best over the next 30-year period. He is able to identify those companies that will produce the highest rate of return on assets. While he cannot see into the future as it pertains to the stock price of those companies, he builds a portfolio of the stocks of these companies because he has confidence that these great-performing companies will, obviously, make great investments.

Jane Smith, on the other hand, believes that markets are efficient. She, therefore, bases her strategy on the theory that if the market believes that a group of companies will produce superior results, then it will already have bid up the price of those stocks to reflect those expectations. The stocks of these great companies will, therefore, produce below-average results. Jane, believing that the market will reward her for taking risk, instead buys a passively managed portfolio of the stocks of value or lousy companies. She anticipates the likelihood that on average these companies will continue to be poor performers; but she expects their stocks to provide superior returns, thereby rewarding her for taking risk. Jane believes that markets work. John does not.

I think it is safe to venture that faced with the choice of buying the stocks of "great" companies or buying the stocks of "lousy" companies, most investors would instinctively choose the former.

Let us now jump forward 30 years. How did John's and Jane's investment strategies work out. Who was right? In a sense, they were both right. John's companies produced superior returns, outperforming Jane's companies, on a return on asset basis, by 10.22 percent to 6.65 percent.

When we look at the investment results, however, we get a totally different outcome. Jane's investment in those lousy companies produced an annual rate of return of 15.76 percent. John's investment in those great companies did not produce such great results. John's investments produced an annual return of 10.45 percent. Despite returns on assets over 50 percent greater than that of the lousy companies, the stocks of the great companies provided far lower returns.

If the major purpose of investment research is to determine which companies will be the great performing companies, and if you are 100 percent correct in your analysis yet still produce inferior results, why bother? Why not save the time and the expense and just let the markets reward you for taking risk?

If the theory that markets provide returns commensurate with the amount of risk taken holds true, one should expect to see similar results if Jane invested in a passively managed portfolio consisting of those risky small companies. When one compares the performance of the asset class of small companies with the performance of the large company asset class, one gets the same results produced by the great company-versus-value company comparison. While small companies produced returns on assets about 25 percent below those of large companies (7.5 percent versus 9.37 percent), investment returns on the stocks of small companies exceeded the returns on stocks of large companies by over 25 percent (14.6 percent versus 11.6 percent). This seeming anomaly actually makes our point that markets work. The riskier investment in small companies produced higher returns.[85]

Glamour Versus Value

It gives you a comfortable feeling when your theories hold up no matter what the circumstances. "No matter how you define 'value,' out-of-favor value stocks have outperformed glamour stocks. It does not matter whether glamour is defined as a high ratio of stock price to book value; a high ratio of price to cash flow; a high rate of sales growth; or a high ratio of price to earnings. . . . For the 22-year period ending in April 1989, the average rate of return of glamour stocks was between 9 percent and 13 percent, while the rate of return of unglamorous value stocks was between 16 percent and 20 percent."[86]

Ignoring facts, because they may seem either difficult to believe or against conventional wisdom, does not cause them to cease to exist. Remember that it is not that the glamorous companies will not outperform the value companies; it is that their stocks will underperform because investors, in a sense, "overpay" for growth companies in their search for safe investments. While not actually overpaying, glamour investors do receive relatively lower returns, and value investors receive relatively higher returns. Nothing ventured, nothing gained. Some clichés are worth repeating. That is how they get to be clichés.

A study by Michele Clayton, "In Search of Excellence: the Investor's Viewpoint," compared the performance of "excellent companies" to "unexcellent companies." While covering a relatively short time frame, 1981–1985, the study provides further evidence that while value (unexcellent) companies underperform growth (excellent) companies, value stocks outperform growth stocks. The excellent companies outperformed the unexcellent companies by: 10.74 percent versus 4.77 percent on an asset growth basis; 9.37 percent versus 3.91 percent on a growth in equity basis; 10.65 percent versus 1.68 percent on a return on total capital basis; 12.92 percent versus −15.08 percent on a return on equity basis; and 6.4 percent versus 1.35 percent on a return on sales basis. However, investments in the value companies far outperformed investments in the growth companies, producing $297.50 versus $181.60 for each $100 invested. No matter how we look at it, markets reward for risk. Markets are efficient.[87]

Over Time, There Is Nothing Like Value

If our theory that value stocks provide superior returns to growth stocks is correct, then it should hold true across all market capitalization levels. Heartland Advisors (with data from Prudential Securities, Inc.) studied the period 1976–1996, a period that includes the greatest bull market U. S. stocks have experienced as well as covering a variety of business cycles, inflation experiences, and interest rate environments. In its winter 1996 letter to clients, Heartland's Michael Berry reported that no matter the market capitalization class, value provided superior returns to a growth strategy.

- Small-cap value stocks returned 20.4 percent and out-performed small-cap growth stocks, which returned 18 percent.

- Mid-cap value stocks returned 18 percent and outperformed mid-cap growth stocks, which returned 16.7 percent.

- Large-cap value stocks returned 15.9 percent and out-performed large-cap growth stocks, which returned 12.1 percent.

Another valuable point can be derived from the study: the smaller the market capitalization asset class, the greater the returns. The small-cap asset class outperformed the mid-cap asset class, and the mid-cap asset class outperformed the large-cap asset class. Since the larger capitalization asset classes are less risky, they should and did produce lower returns. Empirical evidence supports the academic theory that risk and returns are related.

Not only did the value asset class provide superior returns across all market capitalization sizes, it provided those returns with a much more attractive risk-to-reward profile. Using a monthly standard deviation as the measure of risk, Heartland found that within each market capitalization class a value strategy produced a lower variability of returns than a growth strategy.

- The standard deviation of the large-cap value stocks was 3.8 percent versus 4.9 percent for the large-cap growth stocks.

- The standard deviation of the mid-cap value stocks was 4.5 percent versus 5.9 percent for the mid-cap growth stocks.

- The standard of deviation for the small-cap value stocks was 5.1 percent versus 6.4 percent for the small-cap growth stocks.

The study also showed that the smaller the asset class, the greater the volatility—once again demonstrating that the markets are efficient.

One of the risks of investing in risky asset classes is that if your investment time horizon is short, the expected outcome, in terms of returns, may not occur. The corollary to that risk is that the longer the investment horizon, the more likely that outcome is to occur. In the same study, Heartland examined various holding periods to determine how likely a value strategy is to outperform either an index or growth strategy. They found that even when the holding period is as short as one year, value strategies are likely to outperform either index or growth strategies. In addition, the longer the holding period, the greater the likelihood that value will prevail. If the holding period was at least eight years, a value strategy outperformed an index strategy over 97 percent of the time and outperformed a growth strategy almost 91 percent of the time. There is a very important lesson here: patience, and the discipline to stick with your investment strategy, are very important elements of a successful investment strategy.

Investors should take note of the fact that all this superior performance for value occurred during the greatest bull market and the longest period of economic growth without a recession in history. If growth stocks can't outperform in this environment, when they were the rage of most investment "experts," market gurus, and the financial press, when exactly should one expect them to outperform? Will they outperform in periods after market peaks? Let's look at the record.

Using price-to-earnings (P/E) ratios as their measure of value versus growth, Heartland compared the average annual returns of low P/E (value) stocks and high P/E (growth) stocks over three-year holding periods, following 13 market tops between 1950 and 1995. Heartland defined low P/E and high P/E, respectively, as the lowest 20 percent and the highest 20 percent of P/Es in the S & P 500 Index. Heartland found that low P/E stocks returned, on average, 7.12 percent for the 13 periods studied—over eight times the return of 0.88 percent produced by the high P/E stocks. Value stocks not only have clearly outperformed growth stocks over the long term, they also have clearly provided a significant advantage, in terms of performance and risk reduction, during bear markets.[88]

One final example on the benefits of value investing. With the superior performance of the large-cap stocks, as represented by the S & P 500 Index, in both 1995 and 1996, investors may have begun to question their asset allocation decisions. My advice: be patient. Markets work, but only over the longer term. Mont Levy and Ed Goldberg of Buckingham Asset Management studied the performance of the four U. S. asset classes of small value, large value, small-cap, and large-cap for the period 1964–1996, a period that covered a vast array of economic conditions. The study covered 29 rolling five- and 24 rolling ten-year periods. They concluded that the small value and large value asset classes dominated the performance charts, finishing first or second among the four asset classes the vast majority of the time. On the other hand, the large-cap asset class finished either first or second only a handful of times over the rolling five-year periods and never once finished first or second over the rolling ten-year periods. The results are unequivocal. The recent superior performance of the large-cap asset class is probably an anomaly, both from an academic and historical empirical perspective.

I hope the lesson you come away with is that the next time your broker, or a friend, calls to recommend that you buy the stock of some "great" company, you will tell him or her, No thanks. Instead, tell that person that you are interested in great investments, not great companies. Vive la difference.

International Markets Produce the Same Results

If the international markets are efficient in pricing for risk, one should see the same results there that the U. S. markets produced. The riskiest asset classes, not the "great companies," should produce the highest returns. For the period 1975–1992, the returns in the international markets from the "risky"—high book-to-market (value)—and small company asset classes both exceeded 20 percent per annum and beat the returns from both the "safe" international glamour (growth) and international large company asset classes, which each returned about 15 percent per annum. Therefore, we know if we seek the highest returns, we should invest, both domestically and internationally, in the same high-risk asset classes. Markets work. It's that simple.[89]

The Value Premium—Are Markets Efficient?

Recently, articles in the financial press have begun to appear that make the case that the markets are inefficient. The foundation of this thesis is that value stocks outperform glamour stocks while exhibiting lower volatility. With volatility being accepted as a measure of risk, as was shown, value stocks are producing higher returns with less risk. This is an apparent inconsistency with the efficient markets theory, which states that in order to achieve greater returns an investor must buy the securities of riskier companies. Professor Robert Haugen of the University of California, Irvine, even wrote a book on the subject: *The New Finance: A Case Against Efficient Markets.* While I clearly agree that a value strategy will outperform a glamour strategy, I do not agree that the markets are inefficient. While volatility is a useful and convenient measure of risk, it is not the only one. The answer to the seeming anomaly of value stocks providing greater returns with lower volatility lies in the cost of capital story I have already discussed. Value stocks are the stocks of risky companies. The prices of these stocks are distressed (and because individual investors are not risk neutral, the stock prices are distressed to a very low level) relative to the stocks of the glamour companies. Investors know that investments in these companies are risky. Therefore, they demand higher returns from value stocks as compensation (an incentive) for owning them. The value premium is a sign that the markets are working in an efficient manner. And, even if Haugen is correct in saying that the markets are inefficient, as far as an investor is concerned, it does not matter, since his conclusion is the same as that of efficient market theorists—value will carry the day.

The "Small-Cap Effect" by Some Accounts a Myth

An argument has been made by Professor Jeremy Siegel that if we ignore the nine-year period of 1975–1983, the small-cap premium disappears.[90] David Booth of DFA has shown that this argument doesn't hold water. The following table contains the relation between market capitalization (a dimension of risk) and average stock returns. The size breaks are by NYSE size ranges. Decile 1 contains the largest 10 percent of NYSE stocks, and decile 10 the smallest. American Stock Exchange (AMEX) stocks are added in 1963 and NASDAQ stocks in 1975, according to their appropriate size decile. Returns are provided by the Center for Research in Security Pricing (CRSP) at the University of Chicago. The size effect can be measured as the difference in returns between deciles. As is shown in the table, during the boom years the size differential was quite large. Even when one throws out those boom years, the annual return premiums are still large— 6.49 percent between deciles 1 and 10, and 4.71 percent between decile 1 and quintile 5 (deciles 9 and 10). The only conclusion one can draw is that the size effect is still substantial, even when one excludes the boom period for small-cap stocks. (One further word of caution: Excluding the boom period and saying that the small-cap effect doesn't exist would be like saying that if you exclude the month of September when he hit 17 home runs, Babe Ruth would not have hit 60 home runs. No one would accept that proposition.)

Average Annual Returns (%) by Capitalization Decile, 1926–1996

	1926–1996 Excluding 1975–1983	1975–1983 Only	1926–1996 All Years
Decile 1	11.01	14.84	11.56
Decile 2	12.64	19.42	13.50
Decile 3	12.37	23.21	13.75
Decile 4	12.93	26.64	14.67
Decile 5	13.82	26.64	15.44
Decile 6	13.19	28.31	15.11
Decile 7	14.11	30.23	16.15
Decile 8	14.23	31.37	16.41
Decile 9	14.84	32.53	17.08
Decile 10	17.50	35.84	19.82
Quintile 5 Deciles 9 and 10	15.72	34.42	18.09
Annual size effects			
D10 minus D1	6.49	21.00	8.26
Q5 minus D1	4.71	19.58	6.53

Source: CRSP

At this point you may be wondering whether I am advocating investing in only the high-risk asset classes of small and value. Investing in these high-risk asset classes is only risky when viewed in isolation. In later chapters I will show how to reduce the risk of investing in them through the building of a broadly diversified global portfolio, using the tenets of Modern Portfolio Theory.

Fixed Income Assets—Risk and Returns

So far I have focused our attention on the equity side of a portfolio; to complete the picture, one needs to develop a strategy for fixed income assets.

As was shown earlier, active management of fixed income portfolios is the same loser's game as for equity portfolios, a fact that was demonstrated in a study that found that actively managed bond funds underperformed their benchmarks by an average of 0.85 percent per annum.[91] That is certainly an expensive price to pay for the privilege of trying to beat the market. It is also evidence that the markets are efficient. Trying to guess the direction of interest rates is the loser's game. Once again, the winner's game is passive management. Buy and hold bonds of the maturity and risk characteristics that meet your risk profile.

Most investors know that the longer the maturity of a bond, the greater its price sensitivity to a given interest rate change (for the same change in interest rates, a 30-year bond will change in price far more than a five-year bond). Since the risk is greater, one would therefore assume that the longer the maturity of a bond, the greater should be the return. Academic research has, however, found some contradictory evidence. While longer maturities are riskier, returns for longer maturities are not consistently greater. In a working paper entitled "Fixed Income Investing" (March 1997), David Plecha of DFA found that for the period 1964–1996, although yields increase as one initially lengthens maturities, this relationship breaks down once one goes beyond five years.

	1-month T-Bills	1-year Rolling T-Bills	5-year T-Notes	Long-term Government Bonds
Annualized return (%)	6.49	7.46	7.77	7.32
Annualized standard deviation	1.28	2.10	6.58	11.48

Investors in long-term bonds are not compensated for the greater risk they are taking (using standard deviation as a measure of risk). I believe that there is a good explanation for this seeming risk/return anomaly. There are many investors, such as pension plans, that have fixed long-term obligations. In order to create a match between the term of their defined liabilities (the pension obligations due to past and current employees) and the term of their assets (thereby *eliminating* risk), they are willing to accept the price risk of the assets themselves. The investor demand for these longer maturity bonds exceeds the demand by issuers for liabilities of that length. Prices rise (and yields fall) when demand exceeds supply. In this case, the price of long-term bonds has risen sufficiently to make them bad investments for those investors not needing them to match a liability of similar length.

The winning strategy would be to not purchase fixed income assets where the higher risk of a longer maturity is not compensated for by higher returns. As the table indicates, this occurs at five years on the maturity spectrum. Fixed income instruments with this maturity have historically produced returns of 7.77 percent with a standard deviation of 6.58 percent. Standard deviation is a measure of volatility, or risk. (I will explain more about this measure of risk in the next chapter.) The level of risk on a long-term bond is almost twice as great (11.4 percent versus 6.58 percent), yet the returns are 0.45 percent lower. Since investing any further out than five years produces lower returns with higher risk, we know that for the fixed income portion of a portfolio we should not buy any asset with a maturity beyond five years (unless, like the pension funds just discussed, an investor places a priority on matching the maturity of assets with the maturity of liabilities).

In his paper David Plecha provided another rationale for investing in short-term bonds; he found that they have a much lower correlation of returns with equities than do long-term bonds (I will discuss the importance of the correlation of returns in chapter 6). From the perspective of risk reduction, short-term investing is far more effective than long-term investing.

Summary

At this point you have been exposed to most of the theory and facts behind the winning investment strategy. We know that if we want high returns, we buy high-risk asset classes. Conversely, if we are unwilling to accept a high degree of risk, we accept lower returns and invest in low-risk securities such as treasury bills or short-term bonds; or, as I will discuss in later chapters, we can combine asset classes in a way that will achieve a level of risk anywhere in between the two extremes.

If we seek high returns, we start with a preference for equities over bonds. Within the equity asset class, we know to buy the stocks of small companies and lousy, or value, companies. We know to buy and hold passively managed mutual funds that buy all those stocks that fall within our chosen asset class. Within the fixed income asset class, we purchase short-term, not long-term, bonds.

I promised early in the book that you would not need an MBA to understand the Nobel Prize–winning body of work called Modern Portfolio Theory. I have now covered two of the three major tenets of that body of work:

- The markets are efficient. This condition makes active management a loser's game and passive management the winning strategy.

- Add asset class investing to the passive approach. Buying growth companies and large companies is the low-return strategy; buying small companies and value companies is the high-return strategy. Finally, avoid long-term fixed income investments, since they do not provide higher returns, despite entailing greater risk.

With this knowledge, financial economists have built a model that demonstrates that the vast majority of the returns that one can expect a portfolio to generate are determined by the percentage of assets allocated to each of five factors (or asset classes). This paradigm is known as the five-factor model; in the next chapter I will show how this model works and how you can put it to work for you.

CHAPTER 5

◆

The Five-Factor Model

Knowledge is power. —Thomas Hobbes, *Leviathan*

Baseball scouts, when sent to look at the latest hot prospect, are trained to evaluate a player's skills in five areas; speed, throwing arm, fielding, batting, and hitting with power. How a prospect rates in these five skills has proven to be an excellent predictor of whether or not he will make it to the major leagues.

Similarly, financial economists have discovered that there are five factors that determine the vast majority of expected returns from a portfolio. Three factors are related to the portion of the portfolio that is allocated to equities, and two factors are related to fixed income assets. When one combines these into the five-factor model, one can determine the expected return of a balanced equity and fixed income portfolio. I will first examine the three-factor equity model. In succeeding chapters I will show how this model is used to build portfolios.

The Three-Factor Equity Model

The fundamental concept of risk and return in equity investing is embodied in what economists call the three-factor model, which states that the returns one can expect from an equity portfolio are unrelated to either the ability to pick stocks or to time the market. Instead, the degree of exposure to three risk factors determines returns. (As used here, "returns" refers to premiums above the benchmark risk-free rate of return on short-term U. S. treasury bills, i.e., very short-term government obligations that have neither credit nor interest rate risk, hence the term "risk-free.")

The first risk factor in the three-factor equity model is the amount of exposure to equities—the percentage of assets allocated to them. Since equities are riskier than fixed income investments, they should provide greater returns. In fact, they have returned a 5.55 percent (or about 5 percent) premium over the risk-free treasury bill benchmark.

The second risk factor is concerned with the size of a company as determined by market capitalization. The small company asset class, those in the ninth and tenth decile of companies, being a riskier asset class than large companies (deciles 1–5), also have provided a return premium over the risk-free rate of 4.94 percent (or about 5 percent).

The third risk factor takes value into consideration. High book-to-market (value) stocks, being riskier than low book-to-market (growth) stocks also have provided a return premium over the risk-free rate of 5.34 percent (again about 5 percent).

It is important to note that in the international markets both the high book-to-market (value over growth) and size (small over large) risk premiums over the risk-free rate have also been about 5 percent.[92]

The aforementioned risk premiums were determined by isolating each factor; they can then be added together. The risk premium (above the risk-free benchmark of treasury bills) for small capitalization stocks is the sum of the premium for equities in general (5 percent) and the small-cap premium (5 percent), or about 10 percent. The premium for value stocks is the total of the general equities premium (5 percent) and the value premium (5 percent), or about 10 percent. Taking this one step further, the premium for small-cap value stocks is equal to the sum of the premiums for all three risk factors, or about 15 percent.

The following example will help clarify how this three-factor model can be used to project the most likely long-term returns from a portfolio. Keep in mind that the key operative words are "likely" and "long-term." Since all return factors are premiums above the risk-free rate, one must make an assumption about the future return from holding a risk-free instrument, namely treasury bills.

Let us assume that over our investment horizon we expect the return from holding treasury bills will average 5 percent. With this starting point, we can project the likelihood that equity investments will provide per annum returns of 10 percent (5 percent for the risk-free rate + 5 percent for equities). The portions of the portfolio allocated to small-cap and value stocks can each be projected to provide per annum returns of 15 percent (5 percent for the risk-free rate + 5 percent for equities + 5 percent for either small-cap or value stocks). Finally, the portion of the portfolio allocated to small-value stocks can be projected to provide a per annum return of about 20 percent (5 percent for the risk-free rate + 5 percent for equities + 5 percent for small-cap stocks + 5 percent for value stocks). If the risk-free return on treasury bills turns out to be lower than our projection, we should expect all returns to be commensurately lower. Conversely, treasury bill rates that are higher than expected will raise projected returns.

One might conclude from this example that investors concerned only about achieving the highest expected long-term rate of return should invest solely in small-cap value stocks. In fact, this strategy will probably produce the highest returns, since it achieves the greatest exposure to risk. I would, however, caution any investor thinking of adopting this strategy, because asset classes move in and out of "favor" in the financial markets. Investors thinking of adopting this strategy should only do so if they are prepared to endure periods of five years, or possibly longer, during which their portfolio will underperform those with less exposure to risk. This single asset class portfolio is also likelier to be more volatile than a broader diversified portfolio. With this knowledge, each investor can make the decision that best suits his or her unique tolerance for risk and ability to stay the course.

Now that you understand the risk factors that determine expected returns, always remember that beating the market, when the market is defined as the S & P 500, is not difficult. Since the S & P 500 represents the stocks of the largest U. S. companies, an investor in the S & P 500 asset class can expect to receive the risk-free rate of return plus the equity premium. This investor is missing out, however, on the risk premiums of small companies and value companies. Keep this in mind as I relate this next tale.

Fortune reporter Terence Pare claimed, "The truth is that you can beat the market. A claim like that goes straight to the infamous efficient market theory like a stake to a vampire's heart."[93] Mr. Pare uses "infamous" in a way that implies that passive management, resulting from the efficient markets theory, is almost un-American. Investors reading this statement would be led to believe that active management actually works. Unfortunately for Mr. Pare, and his readers, he just doesn't get it; he was comparing apples to oranges. Beating the market (the S & P 500) is simple, as you just learned. All you have to do is load up a portfolio with stocks from the high-risk asset classes of small companies and value companies; you will then be compensated for accepting higher risk with higher returns, just as the efficient markets theory says. Thus, active managers should be judged not against the S & P 500 but against a passively managed asset class benchmark. In other words, a small-cap active manager should be judged against a small-cap index, or a small-cap passively managed fund, an active manager investing in value stocks should be judged against a value benchmark, and so on. When put to this test, statistics show that active managers fail badly because the markets are efficient. Remember: Beware of all claims that active managers can beat the market. What Mr. Pare really should consider as infamous is that despite his claims about being able to beat the market, 70 percent or more of active managers regularly underperform the S & P 500.

Now that you are familiar with the three factors that determine the returns that can be expected from an equity portfolio, I will explain the two factors that determine the returns that can be expected from a fixed income portfolio.

The Two-Factor Fixed-Income Model

Financial economists have determined that there are just two factors that determine the returns that can be expected from a fixed income portfolio. As noted earlier, neither of these two factors have anything to do with the ability to predict the direction of interest rates. The underperformance of bond mutual funds provides clear evidence that trying to time fixed income investments based on predictions of the future direction of interest rates is just as much a loser's game as trying to select individual stocks or time equity investments. Passive management is the winning strategy. The real question that faces fixed income investors is the same one that faces equity investors: How much risk are you willing to accept in search of higher returns? The answer to this question will determine the allocation between instruments of short-term and long-term maturity within the fixed income portion of the portfolio.

The two fixed-income risk factors are maturity and default (or credit risk). The fixed-income model works in the same way as the equity model. We begin with the risk-free rate of return, the rate of return on short-term U. S. government obligations (treasury bills). These instruments, once again, carry neither credit nor interest rate risk. The risk premium for investing in longer term securities is about 1.5 percent. If an investor is willing to buy a five-year treasury note, instead of a one-month treasury bill, that investor will be rewarded for taking the risk of longer term investing with a return premium of about 1.5 percent.

The premium for taking the risk of investing in investment grade corporate debt instruments (versus U. S. government, U. S. government agency, or what are called GSEs—government sponsored entities such as Fannie Mae or Freddie Mac), at least for bond mutual funds, has historically been very close to zero. This calculation is based on comparing the results of long-term government bond funds and long-term corporate bond funds. While corporate bonds carry higher note rates than do government issues, the incremental yield has historically been offset by credit losses, probably higher expense ratios (resulting from the need to analyze the credit risk of corporate issuers), and other features incorporated into corporate bonds, such as a call. A call gives the right to the issuer to call in (prepay) the bonds. The issuer will do so if interest rates drop sufficiently to warrant the expense of the recall and reissuance of new bonds at the then-prevailing lower rate. The investor in such a security, having the high-yielding bond paid off, will then have to purchase a new bond at the new lower rates. No such feature exists in the treasury bond market. The conclusion I draw from this data is that one should invest only in government issues and noncallable investment grade (AA or better) corporate issues. You are just not getting compensated enough to invest in either lower investment grade corporate instruments or callable debt. Since it is unlikely that an individual investor could construct an adequately diversified bond portfolio, the solution is to invest in a passively managed fund that purchases only such instruments. Another conclusion can be drawn: If you want to extract the risk premium for investing in low-grade (high-yield) corporate instruments (i.e., junk bonds) you are far better off owning the stocks of the issuing companies than their bonds.

We can now project the returns from a fixed income portfolio. Once again, we begin with an assumption about the future risk-free rate of return. If we assume, for example, that the risk-free rate will be 5 percent, then we can expect that our short-term fixed income investments will yield 5 percent and our longer term fixed income investments will yield about 6.5 percent.

The Five-Factor Portfolio Model

By combining the three-factor equity model and the two-factor fixed income model, we can now project the expected returns from a balanced portfolio. A simple example will help pull this information together. Assume that an investor decides on a portfolio that has a 50 percent allocation to equities and a 50 percent allocation to fixed income assets. Based on the investor's risk profile, the decision is made to allocate the equity portion to 10 percent large-cap stocks (which provide an equity risk premium of about 5 percent), 10 percent to small-cap stocks (which provide a small company premium of about 5 percent), 10 percent to value stocks (which provide a value company premium of about 5 percent), and 20 percent to small-cap value stocks. (Remember that risk premiums are additive.) The 50 percent fixed income portion is allocated 25 percent to short-term instruments (that carry no risk premium) and 25 percent to long-term instruments (that carry a risk premium of about 1.5 percent). One can now project the long-term rate of return, above the risk-free rate of return, that this portfolio can be expected to generate.

Asset Class	Allocation	× Risk Premium	= Premium Return to Portfolio
Large-cap	10%	5.0%	0.5%
Small-cap	10%	10.0%	1.0%
Value	10%	10.0%	1.0%
Small-cap value	20%	15.0%	3.0%
Short-term fixed	25%	0.0%	0.0%
Long-term fixed	25%	1.5%	0.4%
Total Portfolio			5.9%

We can now project that this portfolio will generate long-term returns above the risk-free rate of about 6 percent (5.9 percent). If the short-term treasury bill rate averages 3 percent over the long term, we can reasonably expect that this portfolio will generate a rate of return of about 9 percent. If the treasury rate averages 5 percent, we would expect this portfolio to return about 11 percent.

Summary

We can project the expected long-term rate of return of a portfolio by examining its exposure to the five dimensions, or factors, of risk. This capacity is one of the major benefits of passive asset class investing. Investing with active managers means you cannot make projections about future returns, since you do not know in which asset classes they will choose to invest.

Our next step is to learn how to construct a portfolio that fits an individual's unique tolerance for risk—the third and last tenet of Modern Portfolio Theory. I will explain all one needs to know about building just such a portfolio in the following chapters.

CHAPTER 6

◆

Volatility, Return, and Risk

Everything has a moral, if only you can find it.
—Lewis Carroll, *Alice's Adventures in Wonderland*

I have already discussed how the risk factors of equities, size, value, maturity, and credit quality impact returns. There is another risk factor one needs to understand before we can implement the winning strategy: how volatility can impact returns. One needs to understand how to control that impact because it is powerful.

Volatility and Returns

Statistics are like a bikini. What they reveal is suggestive, but what they conceal is vital. —Aaron Lowenstein

To illustrate the impact of volatility on a portfolio, let's look at a hypothetical example. Suppose you were offered the choice between two portfolios, one with an average annual return of 15 percent and one with an average annual return of 12 percent. I am sure that the vast majority of people, if not everyone, would not even think twice before choosing the portfolio with the 15 percent annual average return. Surprisingly, the better approach is first to determine the volatility of the two portfolios. Before I explain why, you must first understand how standard deviation is used as a measure of risk.

Standard deviation, a statistical term, is used to measure volatility. It is not a difficult concept to understand. St. Louis and Honolulu might have the same average temperature. However, the standard deviation, or variability, of the temperature in St. Louis is far greater than it is in Honolulu. In terms of investing, standard deviation measures the amount by which annual returns vary, or deviate, from average returns. The greater the variability, the higher the standard deviation. For example, a portfolio with a 15 percent annual average return and an annual standard deviation of 35 percent can be expected to generate annual returns between a negative 20 percent (15 − 35) and a positive 50 percent (15 + 35) in 13 out of every 20 years (about two-thirds of the time). A portfolio with a 12 percent annual average return and an annual standard deviation of 15 percent can be expected to generate annual returns between a negative 3 percent (12 − 15) and a positive 27 percent (12 + 15) in those same 13 out of every 20 years. Clearly the portfolio with the 15 percent annual return is much more volatile, or risky. You can see why standard deviation is used as the measure of risk.

Surprisingly, despite the fact that the average annual rate of return on the first portfolio (15 percent) exceeded the average annual return of the second portfolio (12 percent), it only produced a compounded growth rate of each dollar invested of 9 percent, as compared to 11 percent for the second portfolio. As shown in the following table, over a 20-year period, each dollar invested in the first portfolio grew to $5.49, while each dollar invested in the second portfolio grew to $7.85. The explanation for this anomaly is the higher volatility of this portfolio. Put simply, volatility reduces returns.

Effect of Volatility

Average annual return	15%	12%
Standard deviation	35%	15%
Compound growth rate	9%	11%
Grown of each dollar invested	$5.49	$7.85

Using a simpler example, let's compare two portfolios with exactly the same average annual return but with different standards of deviation.

John Doe's portfolio increases 50 percent one year, decreases 50 percent the next, and then repeats the pattern. Jane Smith's portfolio never increases or decreases in value (she might be holding cash). Both portfolios provide average annual returns of zero. Since both portfolios show the same average return, you would expect that at the end of a four-year period, John and Jane would have portfolios of equal value at the end of the period. You may be surprised to see that the result is quite a bit different. Assuming they both began with $100, John's original investment would grow in the first year to $150, decline in the second to $75, increase in the third to about $112, and decline in the fourth to about $56. Since Jane's portfolio never varied, her $100 investment has held its original value. The 50 percent standard deviation of John's portfolio negatively impacted the outcome. You can clearly see how volatility negatively affects returns. This is important information that one can use to one's advantage when building a portfolio, as I will show.

In yet another example, two portfolios have much closer standard deviations. John Doe's portfolio increases 20 percent one year and then has no growth in the second year. This portfolio has an average annual return of 10 percent and a standard deviation of 10 percent. Jane Smith's portfolio also averages an annual return of 10 percent, but because it increases 10 percent every year its standard deviation is zero. After the first year, John's original investment will grow to $120; it will remain there the second year. Jane's investment will grow to $110 after the first year and to $121 after the second. Once again, the portfolio with the lower standard deviation produced higher growth.

These two examples point out the powerful impact that volatility can have on a portfolio and the relative unimportance of "average annual rates of return." Investors can't spend average rates of return. What should be of greatest concern to investors is the compound growth rate of an invested dollar. Next time you read an ad for a mutual fund, check to see if they are disclosing the average annual return or the compound growth rate of each invested dollar. The latter is the real gauge of a fund's performance and the only way to compare that performance to any other's.

If an investor can find a way to reduce the volatility of a portfolio, the return of that portfolio can be increased. The solution to this problem was provided by Harry Markowitz; it was a major part of his contribution to the 1990 Nobel Prize. It is also the third major tenet of Modern Portfolio Theory.

I will now explain how investors can reduce the volatility of a portfolio, thereby improving the risk/return trade-off—one of the few cases where you can eat your cake and have it too. You can increase your returns without increasing your risk or, conversely, you can reduce risk without having to accept lower returns. In fact, you will learn that despite what you have always heard, there is a free lunch: diversification.

Diversification of Risk

*There are two times in a man's life when he should not speculate:
when he can't afford it, and when he can.*
—Mark Twain, *Following the Equator*

Every investor is familiar with the saying, Don't put all your
eggs in one basket. No matter how good an investment seems,
few individuals would construct a portfolio that consists of just
one asset. Even if one believes that the risk of being wrong is
very small, the cost of being wrong is too great to make that big a
bet. Conversely, even when the odds are stacked against them, as
at the race track or in a lottery, individuals will make an "investment" if the cost of being wrong is small. This type of behavior
demonstrates that investors are not risk neutral; in fact, they are
risk averse, and prudent investors spread their investment dollars
across various investment alternatives. This process is called diversification of risk. I will now explore, using four easy steps,
how one can most effectively use the principle of diversification
to reduce risk.

Let's begin with a portfolio that consists of only the stock of
one company, General Motors. Despite the size and strength of
the company, that would be a very risky, and potentially very
volatile, portfolio. In order to reduce the risk of the portfolio, we
need to diversify. We can do so by adding Ford, but this type of
diversification is not very effective because both companies are
susceptible to the same types of business risk. Since both are
likely to respond to changes in the economic environment in a
very similar manner, their stock prices are likely to move in
a highly correlated manner. (If they moved in exact tandem, they
would have a correlation of +1.) Not only are they likely to move
up and down at the same time, but the sizes of their price movements

are likely to be similar (though not exactly the same). While we slightly reduced the risk of our portfolio by adding a second security (whose correlation to the first was something less than +1), we did not really accomplish our objective. That is, not every diversification produces the same benefits.

We can more effectively reduce the risk and the volatility of our portfolio by adding the stocks of companies from different industries, preferably ones that do not respond in exactly the same way to business cycles. Ideally, we would like to find assets with negative correlation—when one is up, the other is down. If they move in exactly the opposite direction, and by exactly opposite amounts, they have a correlation of -1. (If there was no correlation of price movement, the correlation would be 0.) The addition of assets that had such perfect negative correlation would greatly reduce the volatility of our portfolio. Although assets that have negative correlation are hard to find, risk can be reduced by including in a portfolio assets whose correlation is less than $+1$, and the less the better. Since the mathematical explanation of this point is beyond the scope of this book, I will just point out that this discovery, to a great degree, is why Harry Markowitz was awarded the Nobel Prize in 1990. It is also an important part, as you will learn, of Modern Portfolio Theory.

Even without any understanding of the math, I think you can accept that an investor would have reduced the risk of our sample portfolio by adding Merck (a drug company), Citicorp (a financial institution), or A T & T (a communications company) to the portfolio. This type of diversification works because these companies are not susceptible to exactly the same business risks as an automobile manufacturer (e.g., changes in the price of gasoline). The more companies from different industries one adds to the portfolio, the more one reduces its volatility, and therefore its risk.

It is difficult for individual investors to construct an equity portfolio that achieves a broad enough diversification to reduce overall risk to an acceptable level. Fortunately, mutual funds solve this problem. The use of mutual funds is a very efficient method of achieving the required degree of risk diversification. Some mutual funds hold thousands of different securities.

Step 1: Buy mutual funds instead of individual securities.

Further steps are in order. If we bought two or more mutual funds that all invested in the same type of companies (such as technology companies or health care companies), we would make the same mistake as if we bought two automobile manufacturers. And if we bought two or more funds that invested in the same asset class (such as small, large, value, or growth companies), we would make a similar, though not as grievous, mistake. Two funds comprised of securities from the same asset class—groups of companies with similar risk characteristics—tend to move with high degrees of correlation. While we have diversified away (provided insurance against) business risk, we have not diversified away asset class risk. Asset classes move in and out of favor in the securities market. In some years, small companies are the best performers. In other years, value or large companies may rise to the top. The top performing asset class in one year is just as likely to repeat as fall to the bottom. Most important, no one knows which asset class will top the list next year. In order to reduce risk, we need to diversify across a broad group of asset classes.

Step 2: Create a portfolio of mutual funds that is diversified across several asset classes.

Even taking this step would not complete the process of effective diversification. We also need to diversify country or market risk. Investing in only the U. S. market because foreign markets are perceived as risky is similar to the mistake of investing in only the automobile industry. Since the main determinant of the performance of foreign markets is local conditions, foreign markets do not move in perfect correlation to the U. S. market. The following table shows the correlation, on a monthly basis, of foreign markets with the S & P 500 Index since 1991. We know that the addition of asset classes with a correlation of less than +1 will reduce the volatility of a portfolio; the table provides evidence that the addition of foreign securities to a portfolio will provide the benefit of risk reduction. All the countries listed have low correlation with the S & P 500.

Country	Correlation with S & P 500
Britain	0.55
Canada	0.46
France	0.43
Australia	0.42
Germany	0.33
Hong Kong	0.31
Indonesia	0.24
Mexico	0.19
India	0.15
Japan	0.14

Source: *Forbes,* September 30, 1996

Investors who avoid the risk of foreign markets make the mistake of looking at these asset classes in isolation. The addition of risky asset classes to a portfolio, if these asset classes have less than perfect correlation with the rest of the portfolio, can actually reduce its volatility.

To achieve the most effective diversification, our portfolio would include mutual funds that invest not only in the United States but also Europe, the Far East, and emerging markets. The addition of the emerging markets asset class provides particularly strong diversification benefits because the stock markets of emerging market countries have particularly low correlation of returns with the U. S. equity markets.[94] This type of portfolio diversifies not only business risk but also country risk; doing so can dramatically reduce the volatility, and therefore risk, of a portfolio.

Step 3: Include international mutual funds in your portfolio.

In following steps 1–3, remember to buy only mutual funds that are passively managed. As I will show in chapter 9, it is the only way to insure that your portfolio maintains your desired asset allocation.

The next chapter shows you how to build a portfolio that can provide above-market returns. In other words, you will see that passive management does not mean you have to accept "average" returns (and I have shown that the vast majority of active managers provide below-average returns). You will also discover that you can achieve these superior returns without taking greater risk, and you will see how this can be accomplished in six easy steps. Harry Markowitz coined the phrase "the efficient frontier of risk" to describe a portfolio that produces the highest return for a given level of risk (or the lowest level of risk for a given expected return). In other words, diversification is efficient when it allows you to either reduce risk without reducing returns or to increase returns without increasing risk. He built a mathematical model that would find this efficient frontier—another major part of his contribution to Modern Portfolio Theory.

Once you understand how such an efficient portfolio is built, you will be able to build a portfolio that meets your unique investment time horizons and tolerance for risk.

PART THREE

◆

THE WINNER'S GAME
Make Modern Portfolio Theory Work for You

Anybody can win, unless there happens to be a second entry.
—George Ade

CHAPTER 7

◆

Six Steps to a Diversified Portfolio Using Modern Portfolio Theory

Not only is there but one way of doing things rightly, there is but one way of seeing them, and that is seeing the whole of them. —John Ruskin, *The Two Paths*

In baseball the general manager's job is to put together a team that is well balanced between hitting, fielding, pitching, and running speed. If he builds a team with great power but little speed or pitching, it is likely to suffer from too many strikeouts, double plays, and batting slumps to win a championship. If he focuses on pitching and defense, the team probably will be unable to score enough runs to compensate for the days its pitching or defense is poor. While teams that are built around one area of strength may go on brief winning streaks when everything is going right, they are unlikely to win often enough over a long season to be champions. A general manager succeeds by building a team with diversified strengths. Similarly, individual investors succeed by building and properly managing diversified portfolios.

Jonathan Clements, a columnist for the *Wall Street Journal*, noted: "Indexing is a wonderful strategy. It's a shame most folks get it wrong."[95] I agree with his remark. He was referring to his

147

belief that most investors who use index funds limit themselves to funds that mimic the S & P 500 Index. In this chapter, you will see how to expand on a simple S & P 500 indexing strategy and embark on the winning investment strategy by applying the principles of Modern Portfolio Theory. I will demonstrate how an investor can build a strong, diversified investment portfolio by:

- Utilizing only passive asset class mutual funds;

- Utilizing the high return asset classes of small companies and value companies;

- Eliminating the use of long-term debt from the fixed income portion of the portfolio; and

- Utilizing global diversification to improve the efficiency of the portfolio (reduce volatility without reducing returns).

I will demonstrate the power of Modern Portfolio Theory by following the performance of a "control" portfolio, with a traditional asset allocation of 60 percent equities and 40 percent fixed income, over a 20-year period. This 60/40 allocation is typical of the asset allocation of U. S. pension plans, so-called balanced mutual funds, and many individual investors. I will assume that our investor, knowing that active management is a loser's game, will use only passively managed asset class funds.

Since our investor is probably unaware of the benefits of Modern Portfolio Theory, that is, passive asset class investing combined with broad diversification, he purchases an S & P 500 Index fund for his equity allocation and a Lehman Government/Corporate Bond Index fund for his fixed income allocation. The Lehman Government/ Corporate Bond Index is a popular fixed income index that is often used as a benchmark against which active managers are measured.

I will first show how this investor did if he had the patience to stay with this allocation from 1975 to 1995. Then I will determine how he could have improved performance, that is, built a more efficient portfolio, by using broadly diversified passive asset class funds. I will do so in six easy steps, using six variations on the control portfolio, so that you can clearly see Modern Portfolio Theory at work.

Before going through this process, however, there is one other important issue that needs to be discussed—the distinctions and differences between the three types of mutual funds: institutional, institutional-style, and retail.

Institutional Funds

Institutional funds do not accept investments from individual investors. They require their investors to be "institutions," such as pension and profit-sharing plans and endowment funds. This restriction provides certain advantages:

- Their large average account size minimizes expenses.

- Their restricted market limits the need for marketing and advertising expenses, which provide no added value to investors in the fund.

- Institutions are long-term investors with more discipline than retail investors, which allows the institutional fund to stay virtually fully invested because the need to hold low-return cash reserves—to meet potential investor liquidations in the face of market declines—is minimized.

- The more disciplined buy and hold approach of institutional investors allows the institutional fund to minimize trading expenses. Keep in mind that trading costs incurred when new investors add funds are absorbed by existing shareholders, and when existing shareholders withdraw funds, trading costs are absorbed by remaining shareholders.

These four factors allow institutional funds to give their investors the highest return after expenses.

Institutional-style Funds

Institutional-style funds are a relatively new hybrid. Their creation allowed institutional money managers—such as DFA, Bankers Trust, and Barclays Global Investors—to tap a portion of the retail market without the negative impact on returns experienced by retail funds. (I will discuss the negative impact on returns experienced by retail funds shortly.) Although not available to the general public, institutional-style mutual funds can be purchased by individual investors through a select group of Registered Investment Advisors, who are required to educate their clients on the benefits of passive asset class investing and the buy and hold strategy. Their clients must commit to this strategy. While investors can always access their assets, advisors who utilize institutional-style funds educate clients to think of their investments as illiquid, that is, not readily available for redemption. In other words, investment strategies should change only in response to changes in financial or family situations. Through the distribution channel of financial advisors, institutional-style funds are able to attract retail clients without adversely effecting the returns of their institutional clients.

The use of institutional or institutional-style funds is an important part of the investment process.

Retail Funds

Retail-oriented funds are available to the public, either directly or through financial advisors and brokers.

There are five reasons why I recommend institutional-style funds over retail funds.

(1) Institutional and institutional-style funds do not advertise to the general public, but retail funds must advertise in order to attract investors. Many also pay brokers commissions for acquiring clients. These costs diminish the investment returns of retail funds while obviously providing no value to investors in the fund. Investors who watch television or read the financial press can't escape the blitzkrieg of advertising from the retail mutual fund industry. Neuberger & Berman, Fidelity Investments, and Janus are just three of the many large retail mutual fund families that have been dramatically increasing their advertising budgets. One company, MFS Investment Management, is increasing its 1997 ad budget almost 400 percent, from $2.3 million to $10 million. Two-thirds of that increase will go toward a new national TV campaign. One explanation for this explosive growth in marketing expenditures is: "Fund managers are finding it increasingly difficult to beat the market averages, so name recognition serves as another weapon in the battle for customers." According to Roger Carlock, senior vice-president and director of advertising for MFS, "When looking for a fund, you feel better when a company is out there advertising."[96]

I take a different view of advertising expenditures: they do nothing for existing shareholders except reduce returns. Brian Mattes, a spokesman for the Vanguard Group, agreed. "We will maintain our modest advertising budget. We don't think it's appropriate to take shareholders' money to bring in new shareholders."[97]

Lavish advertising budgets are unnecessary; they only reduce shareholder returns.

(2) The lower returns of retail-oriented funds can also be attributed to the smaller average size account, which increases the fund's expense base. While the average U. S. equity fund carries an expense ratio (the operating expenses of the fund that must be subtracted from investment returns in order to calculate the net return the investor receives) of 1.52 percent of assets, the average institutional fund carries an expense ratio of only 0.93 percent. The difference basically accounted for the higher returns provided by institutional funds.[98]

(3) The most important factor that negatively impacts the returns of retail funds is the need to maintain liquidity, in the form of cash or short-term marketable securities, to meet potential investor withdrawal demands. Retail funds typically have an element of "hot" money. Unlike institutional investors, retail fund investors tend to chase the latest hot sector, asset class, or money manager. As a group, individual investors have shorter investment horizons than institutional investors. They also have less discipline in sticking to their investment strategies, particularly when the market experiences a sharp decline. The need for a retail fund to hold even a small percentage of total funds in short-term marketable securities results in reduced returns. For example, assume a retail mutual fund holds 6 percent of its assets in short-term securities, while an institutional fund holds just a 1 percent reserve. If the reserves earn 5 percent during a period when equities are rising 15 percent per annum, the retail fund will underperform by 0.5 percent per annum [(6 percent − 1 percent) × (15 percent − 5 percent)].

(4) Retail funds incur trading expenses (bid–offer spreads and commissions) generated by the buying and selling activity of some of their investors. These trading expenses are borne by all the fund's investors, thereby reducing returns.

(5) The rapid growth of the mutual fund industry over the past decade and the greatest bull market in history have resulted in

almost 90 percent of the funds now invested in mutual funds having never experienced a bear market (the last bear market was the crash of 1987). When the next bear market inevitably arrives, retail investors are far more likely to run for cover and sell than institutional investors, who are more likely to adhere to the allocations stated in their investment policy guidelines. If retail investors flee, their fund's transactions costs will not only rise, but as the fund sells securities (with large gains resulting from the great bull market) to meet investor liquidations, the remaining shareholders will be left with a very large tax bill. Even mutual funds that have been tax-efficient in the past, such as index funds, will see their tax efficiency gone with the wind.

For all these reasons, I recommend investing in institutional-style mutual funds.

The Control Portfolio

Let us now check the 20-year performance of our control portfolio to see how our basic 60 percent equity and 40 percent fixed income allocation performed.

Portfolio 1: Control Portfolio

S & P 500 Index		60%
Lehman Gov't/Corp		40%
	1975–1995	
Annualized Return	*Annualized Standard Deviation*	*Growth of a Dollar*
13.5%	10.5%	$14.39

Source: See "Sources and Descriptions of Data," page 268.

This simple portfolio provided an annualized return of 13.5 percent. Its standard deviation, a measure of volatility, was 10.5 percent. A dollar invested in 1975 grew to $14.39 by the end of 1995, a return that would have satisfied most investors.

By changing the composition of the control portfolio, through a step-by-step process, I will show how the application of Modern Portfolio Theory allows investors to increase their equity allocation, thereby improving returns, without increasing risk from the basic 60/40 strategy.

Step 1: Apply the principle of diversification.

While maintaining the equity allocation at 60 percent, we reduce the allocation to the S & P 500 Index to 45 percent and allocate 15 percent to an EAFE (Europe, Australia, and the Far East large company) Index fund. We maintain our equity allocation of 60 percent but shift the equity portion from 100 percent U. S. to 75 percent U. S. and 25 percent international. This revised allocation produced the following results:

Portfolio 2: The International Effect

S & P 500 Index		45%	
EAFE Index		15%	
Lehman Gov't/Corp		40%	

	Annualized Return	1975–1995 Annualized Standard Deviation	Growth of a Dollar
Portfolio 1	13.50%	10.50%	$14.39
Portfolio 2	13.80%	9.90%	$15.16

Source: See "Sources and Descriptions of Data."

As you can see, we increased the annualized return from 13.5 percent to 13.8 percent, while the volatility of the portfolio actually decreased from 10.5 percent to 9.9 percent. The growth of each dollar invested increased from $14.39 to $15.16. We certainly achieved the objective of increasing the efficiency of our portfolio, since we produced greater returns with lower risk than the control portfolio.

Step 2: Add a small company asset class fund to the portfolio.

With our next step we reduce our S & P 500 (large domestic company) allocation from 45 percent to 30 percent and replace this portion of it with a 15 percent allocation to a U. S. small company fund that owns the smallest 50 percent of U. S. companies ranked by market capitalization. In doing so, we maintain both our 60 percent equity allocation and our 75 percent U. S. allocation.

Portfolio 3: The U. S. Small Company Effect

S & P 500 Index		30%	
U. S. 6–10 small		15%	
EAFE Index		15%	
Lehman Gov't/Corp		40%	

	1975–1995		
	Annualized Return	Annualized Standard Deviation	Growth of a Dollar
Portfolio 1	13.50%	10.50%	$14.39
Portfolio 2	13.80%	9.90%	$15.16
Portfolio 3	14.50%	10.00%	$17.25

Source: See "Sources and Descriptions of Data."

The addition of the higher expected return asset class of small companies increased returns from 13.8 percent to 14.5 percent (a 5 percent increase) while slightly increasing the volatility of the portfolio from 9.9 percent to 10.0 percent (a 1 percent increase). The growth of each dollar invested improved from $15.16 to

$17.25 (a 13.8 percent increase). Although the volatility of this portfolio increased slightly, I believe that most investors would accept this increase in exchange for an improved rate of return. It is worth noting that while the volatility of Portfolio 3 is greater than the volatility of Portfolio 2, its volatility is less than that of the control portfolio.

Step 3: Add the asset classes of small-cap value and large-cap value.

We now split our 15 percent allocation to U. S. small into 8 percent U. S. small and 7 percent U. S. small value, and we split our 30 percent S & P 500 Index (large-cap) allocation into 15 percent S & P 500 Index and 15 percent U. S. large value.

Portfolio 4: The U. S. Value Effect

S & P 500 Index		15%
U. S. large value		15%
U. S. 6–10 small		8%
U. S. small value		7%
EAFE Index		15%
Lehman Gov't/Corp		40%

	1975–1995		
	Annualized Return	Annualized Standard Deviation	Growth of a Dollar
Portfolio 1	13.50%	10.50%	$14.39
Portfolio 2	13.80%	9.90%	$15.16
Portfolio 3	14.50%	10.00%	$17.25
Portfolio 4	15.30%	10.20%	$19.74

Source: See "Sources and Descriptions of Data."

Adding the asset classes of U. S. small value and U. S. large value increases the rate of return from 14.5 percent to 15.3 percent (an increase of 5.5 percent) and increases volatility from 10.0 percent to 10.2 percent (an increase of only 2 percent). The growth of each dollar invested increased from $17.25 to $19.74 (an increase of 14.4 percent). While the volatility of the portfolio slightly increased, I believe that most investors would choose Portfolio 4 because the increase in returns was far greater than the increase in risk. Also worth noting is that the volatility of Portfolio 4 was less than that of the control portfolio.

Step 4: Replace the 15 percent allocation to the EAFE Index fund, which provides a large company exposure to the international markets, with the higher returning asset classes of international value (8 percent) and international small (7 percent). The international exposure, therefore, remains unchanged at 15 percent.

Portfolio 5: The International Small and Value Effect

S & P 500 Index	15%
U. S. large value	15%
U. S. 6–10 small	8%
U. S. small value	7%
International value	8%
International small	7%
Lehman Gov't/Corp	40%

	1975–1995		
	Annualized Return	Annualized Standard Deviation	Growth of a Dollar
Portfolio 1	13.50%	10.50%	$14.39
Portfolio 2	13.80%	9.90%	$15.16
Portfolio 3	14.50%	10.00%	$17.25
Portfolio 4	15.30%	10.20%	$19.74
Portfolio 5	16.30%	9.90%	$23.65

Sources: See "Sources and Descriptions of Data."

This portfolio increased the annualized return from 15.3 percent to 16.3 percent (an increase of 6.5 percent). At the same time, the power of diversification reduced the volatility of the portfolio from 10.2 percent to 9.9 percent (a decrease of 3 percent). The growth of each dollar invested increased from $19.74 to $23.65 (an increase of 19.8 percent). With greater returns and lower risk, we improved the efficiency of our portfolio.

Step 5: Replace the 40 percent allocation to the Shearson Lehman Government/Corporate Bond Index with a 20 percent allocation to a one-year fixed income fund and a 20 percent allocation to a five-year fixed income fund.

We do so because long-term fixed income securities do not appropriately compensate investors for risk.

Portfolio 6: The Short-Term Fixed Income Effect

S & P 500 Index	15%
U. S. large value	15%
U. S. 6–10 small	8%
U. S. small value	7%
International value	8%
International small	7%
One-year fixed	20%
Five-year fixed	20%

1975–1995

	Annualized Return	Annualized Standard Deviation	Growth of a Dollar
Portfolio 1	13.50%	10.50%	$14.39
Portfolio 2	13.80%	9.90%	$15.16
Portfolio 3	14.50%	10.00%	$17.25
Portfolio 4	15.30%	10.20%	$19.74
Portfolio 5	16.30%	9.90%	$23.65
Portfolio 6	16.10%	8.70%	$23.10

Source: See "Sources and Descriptions of Data."

The shift from long-term fixed income investments to shorter term fixed income investments has a very positive effect on the volatility of the portfolio, with very little impact on returns.

Volatility of the portfolio decreased from 9.9 percent to 8.7 percent (a decrease of 12.1 percent), while returns decreased slightly from 16.3 percent to 16.1 percent (a decrease of 1.2 percent). The growth of each dollar invested only declined from $23.65 to $23.10 (a decrease of 2.3 percent). Considering the dramatic decrease in volatility, with only a slight decrease in returns, I am sure most investors would prefer Portfolio 6 to Portfolio 5.

At this point it is worth comparing the control portfolio to Portfolio 6. Despite maintaining our equity/fixed allocation at 60 percent/40 percent, we managed to increase our rate of return from 13.5 percent to 16.1 percent (an increase of 19.2 percent). We accomplished this increase in returns while actually decreasing the volatility, or risk, of our portfolio from 10.5 percent to 8.7 percent (a decrease of 17.1 percent). The growth of each dollar invested grew from $14.39 to $23.10 (an increase of 60.5 percent). We accomplished these once seemingly incompatible objectives by applying the principles of Modern Portfolio Theory—that is, adding the higher returning asset classes of small and value together with broad global diversification.

Step 6: Increase the equity allocation from 60 to 70 percent and reduce the fixed income portion from 40 to 30 percent, keeping our U. S./international allocation at 75 percent/25 percent.

By increasing the equity allocation from 60 percent to 70 percent, we are able to significantly improve returns. Even more noteworthy is that Portfolio 7 produced the highest rate of return, while only Portfolio 6 experienced lower volatility, with a standard deviation of 8.7 percent versus 9.9 percent. The benefits of diversification, in terms of reduced volatility, far exceeded the risk implications of being invested in the higher returning asset classes of small-cap and value.

One would expect investors to choose Portfolio 7 over Portfolios 1–5, because it is the most efficient of the group; it produced higher returns without increased risk. This decision leaves an investor to choose between Portfolio 6 and Portfolio 7. While Portfolio 7 outperformed Portfolio 6 by 17.2–16.1 percent, it did so while incurring greater volatility; it produced 6.8 percent greater returns than Portfolio 6 but experienced 13.8 percent greater volatility. The choice between portfolios will vary according to each investor's tolerance for risk; either choice can be correct.

Portfolio 7: The Effect of an Increased Equity Allocation

S & P 500 Index	17%
U. S. large value	16%
U. S. 6–10 small	10%
U. S. small value	9%
International value	9%
International small	9%
One-year fixed	15%
Five-year fixed	15%

	Annualized Return	Annualized Standard Deviation	Growth of a Dollar
		1975–1995	
Portfolio 1	13.50%	10.50%	$14.39
Portfolio 2	13.80%	9.90%	$15.16
Portfolio 3	14.50%	10.00%	$17.25
Portfolio 4	15.30%	10.20%	$19.74
Portfolio 5	16.30%	9.90%	$23.65
Portfolio 6	16.10%	8.70%	$23.10
Portfolio 7	17.20%	9.90%	$28.15

Source: See "Sources and Descriptions of Data."

Does Passive Investing Produce Average Returns?

Through the process of building our model portfolios, it becomes clear that the major criticism of passive portfolio management—that it produces average returns—is just not true. A portfolio whose sole asset was an S & P 500 Index fund produced a return of 14.6 percent per annum, with a standard deviation of 13.7 percent, for the 20-year period ending in 1995. As noted earlier, the vast majority of mutual funds underperformed this portfolio, even on a pretax basis. Portfolio 6, with only a 60 percent equity allocation, produced annual returns of over 16 percent, with a standard deviation of under 9 percent. Portfolio 7, with a 70 percent equity allocation, produced annual returns of over 17 percent, with a standard deviation of under 10 percent. Since the vast majority of professional managers underperformed the 14.6 percent annual return of the S & P 500 Index portfolio, it would be difficult for anyone to argue that 16–17 percent returns were average, particularly since these returns were produced with reduced volatility. Had we built a portfolio with a 100 percent equity allocation (providing an apples to apples comparison with the S & P 500 Index portfolio), we would obviously have produced even higher returns than produced by our 70 percent/30 percent portfolio.

Let's quickly review. First, markets are efficient. With this understanding, we concluded that attempts to either select individual securities that were undervalued or to time the market would be nonproductive. Therefore, we chose a passive management approach. We then identified the asset classes that would produce the highest returns and saw that because the markets are efficient at pricing for risk, the highest returning asset classes are those that have the highest risk. These asset classes were small capitalization companies and value companies. We showed how to spread risk by owning a large number of these companies (all companies within the given asset class) through the purchasing of passive asset class funds. Finally, we saw how to lower risk and improve the risk/reward trade-off by diversifying across a broad spectrum of asset classes, including international.

In the next chapter we will explore several different model portfolios. We will start with a conservative portfolio and gradually add risk and return. I will then provide an investment approach that will help you choose the portfolio that best meets your objectives and your tolerance for risk.

CHAPTER 8

♦

How to Build a Model Portfolio

Fortune favors the bold. —Virgil, *Aeneid*

It's Super Bowl Sunday, you are the head coach of one of the combatants, and your team is trailing 17–14. The good news is that your team has the ball on the opponent's one-yard line. But it's fourth down, and only one second is left on the clock. Do you play it safe and kick the tying field goal to send the game into overtime, or do you go for broke and try for the winning touchdown? Many questions rush through your mind. How much confidence do I have in my offense? If we kick the field goal, can my defense hold the opponent if they win the coin toss? Even a field goal isn't a sure thing. Which is the correct decision?

Different coaches will come to different conclusions based on their assessments of such questions. Perhaps the deciding factor will be the personality of the coach. The extent to which the coach is a risk taker may ultimately force the decision between kicking the field goal or going for glory.

Choosing an appropriate asset allocation when creating an

investment portfolio is, in many ways, like the decision facing the Super Bowl coach. First, there is no right answer. Many factors, such as investment time horizon, play a part in the decision-making process. A major determinant should be the ability to accept and deal with the possibility of a negative outcome. In football, the price of going for the glory is the possibility of living with the agony of defeat. In the field of investments, the price of seeking high returns is the possibility, if not probability, of accepting long periods of poor or even negative returns.

How does an investor choose a portfolio that will meet his or her unique tolerance for risk and unique time horizon? To show how to do so, I will explore several different model portfolios, starting with a conservative approach and then gradually adding risk and return to the portfolio.

I will examine four model portfolios and discuss how they performed over a recent 23-year period. The portfolios will range in their equity allocation from 20 percent to 80 percent and be characterized as: Defensive (20 percent equity/80 percent debt); Conservative (40 percent equity/60 percent debt); Moderate (60 percent equity/40 percent debt); and Aggressive (80 percent equity/ 20 percent debt). These categories should cover the risk spectrum of most investors. Then I will examine the annual compound returns and standard deviations of these portfolios. I will also look at the worst single year and the worst single three-year period occurring during the 23-year history. These two measurements are to be used as the benchmarks against which an investor can measure his or her willingness and ability to absorb the "stomach acid" these periods produce. Finally, I will examine the growth of each dollar invested if the investor stayed the course and rebalanced the portfolio at the end of each year in order to maintain the chosen percentage allocation to each asset class.

You will note that in building the model portfolios four additional equity asset classes have been added to the higher risk asset classes of small, value, and small value. The first additional equity asset class is real estate; the portfolio within this asset class consists largely of income-producing real estate, usually in the form of real estate investment trusts (REITs). Real estate is added to our asset class mix for its diversification benefit (real estate assets tend to perform well in periods of high inflation when other asset classes are performing poorly) as well as the returns real estate investments provide for accepting the risks involved in them. When building your own portfolio, remember that if you own a home, you already have a portion of your portfolio allocated to the real estate asset class. You may wish to take this into account when deciding on your asset allocation.

The second additional equity asset class is emerging markets; this asset class consists of stocks of established companies in nine of the world's emerging economies—Argentina, Brazil, Indonesia, Israel, Malaysia, Mexico, Portugal, Thailand, and Turkey. These countries have approximately equal weighting in the portfolio in order to provide the broadest possible diversification of country risk. Since investing in the markets of these countries is considered more risky than investing in the markets of developed countries, emerging market investments should provide returns that adequately compensate for that excess risk. In fact, they have done just that. Over the 50-year period 1945–1995, emerging markets equities produced annual returns of 16.5 percent, compared with 12.4 percent for the S & P 500 Index and 11.8 percent for the EAFE Index.[99] Once again, we see that markets work. Investors who accept greater risk are rewarded with greater returns.

The third and fourth additional equity asset classes are large-capitalization U.S. stocks and large-capitalization international stocks. While these asset classes have not proven to be the highest returning asset classes, they do add value because of their diversification benefits. While the positive relationship between risk and return becomes more certain as we extend the investment time frame, high-risk asset classes can provide subpar returns for periods of up to five years or even longer. In addition, since large-cap stocks have demonstrated some degree of noncorrelation with the movement of small cap and value stocks, their addition to our model portfolios will reduce the volatility of these portfolios. Therefore, in order to reduce risk, we add to our model portfolios an allocation of both U.S. and international large-cap stocks. (Aggressive investors may choose to exclude large-cap stocks from their portfolio, trading somewhat higher volatility for higher expected returns.)

I have also added one fixed income asset class to the model portfolio: global fixed income, which consists of bonds from seven major developed countries. Since the fixed income markets of these seven countries do not all rise or fall at the same time, we receive the benefit of reduced volatility. The assets within this fund, unlike those in our international equity funds, are fully hedged against currency risk.

I will explore how our four model portfolios performed over the period 1973–1995. This analysis intentionally includes an additional two years from our previous seven portfolios to make sure we include 1973–1974, the two worst investment years since the depression. Including these years allows us to see the performance of our portfolios in the worst of times as well as the best of times. This information is particularly relevant to investors who find it easy to stick with an investment plan when everything is going well but have more difficulty doing so in bear markets.

How Much to Allocate to International Equities?

Before I explore portfolio alternatives, I would like to offer some insights about the allocation of equity investments between domestic and international asset classes. Not long ago, the U.S. equity markets constituted about three-fourths of the total capitalization of global equities. Today that number is much closer to one-third. Since many investment advisors recommend that asset allocations be determined by a particular country's share of the global equity markets, this would result in a U.S. investor's international allocation being as high as two-thirds of the portfolio. Although there is some logic to this argument, such a large allocation completely ignores what is known as event risk—the possibility of an unanticipated occurrence. In recent history, major events, such as World Wars I and II and the Communist takeover of Cuba, resulted in the total loss or confiscation of U.S. investments in certain foreign countries. With this possibility in mind, note that these model portfolios do not include an international allocation greater than 30 percent. Aggressive investors, aware of event risk, might wish to choose a higher international allocation. In deciding on your emerging markets allocation, keep in mind that while this is a high-return asset class, it is also one that is especially sensitive to event risk. If there is a change in the local political climate (as frequently occurs in emerging markets countries), the emerging market may become a submerging market. The possibility of a submerging market is why our model portfolios do not include an emerging markets allocation exceeding 6 percent. Once again, aggressive investors, willing to accept event risk, may choose a higher allocation.

Model Portfolios
1973–1995

	Defensive	Conservative	Moderate	Aggressive
Equity (%)	20	40	60	80
U.S. stocks (%)	10	20	35	50
Large-cap (%)	2	4	10	15
Large-cap value(%)	2	4	10	15
Small-cap (%)	2	4	5	8
Small-cap value (%)	2	4	5	7
Real estate (%)	2	4	5	5
International stocks (%)	10	20	25	30
Value (%)	4	8	0	8
Large-cap (%)	0	0	10	8
Small-cap (%)	3	6	10	8
Emerging markets (%)	3	6	5	6
Fixed income (%)	80	60	40	20
U.S. 5-year gov't (%)	20	15	10	5
U.S. 1-year gov't (%)	40	30	20	10
Global fixed income (%)	20	15	10	5
Compound return (%)	11.4	13.1	14.1	14.9
Standard deviation (%)	5.8	8.7	11.7	14.8
Lowest 1-year return (%)	0.0	−9.8	−18.5	−27.0
Lowest 3-year return (%)	6.5	4.3	2.3	0.0
Growth of a dollar	$11.90	$16.80	$20.90	$24.60

Source: See "Sources and Descriptions of Data," page 268.

An investor who chose the Defensive portfolio achieved a very respectable 11.4 percent per annum compounded rate of return and experienced a standard deviation of only 5.8 percent per annum.

Most important, despite enduring the two worst years for the stock market since the depression, the portfolio never incurred a loss. In addition, the worst three-year period resulted in a gain of 6.5 percent. Finally, each dollar invested grew to $11.90.

Moving all the way to the right, an investor who chose the Aggressive portfolio achieved an annual compound rate of return of 14.9 percent, 3.5 percent per annum better than the performance of the Defensive portfolio. The higher return, however, came at the expense of a greater standard deviation—14.8 percent per annum—almost three times that of the Defensive portfolio. This outcome is not unexpected. Over the long term, greater risk should be accompanied by greater reward for accepting that risk. Unlike the Defensive portfolio, which never experienced a loss, the Aggressive portfolio incurred a loss of 27 percent in its single worst year; it also took three years just to get back to zero. The real compensation for enduring the "stomach acid" of those bad periods was that each dollar invested eventually grew to $24.60, over twice the result achieved by the Defensive portfolio. Markets reward risk taking. As John Maynard Keynes said: "In the main, therefore, slumps are experiences to be lived through . . . with as much equanimity and patience as possible."[100]

The Conservative and Moderate portfolios also produced returns and standard deviations that were reflective of their levels of risk. How should the individual investor choose the portfolio that is right for him or her? I recommend that an investor go through two tests—the stomach acid test and the liquidity test.

The Stomach Acid Test

Your ultimate success or failure will depend on your ability to ignore the worries of the world long enough to allow your investments to succeed. It isn't the head, but the stomach that determines [your] fate. —Peter Lynch, *Beating the Street*

The "stomach acid" tests ask the question, "Do you have the fortitude and discipline to stick with your predetermined investment strategy (asset allocation) when the going gets rough?" At some point, it will certainly get rough. Successful investment management depends to a large degree on the ability of an individual to withstand the periods of stress, and on his or her ability to endure the severe emotional challenges present during bear markets. In order to achieve the superior returns of the Aggressive portfolio, you would not only have to endure the negative 27 percent year, but you would also need the courage to buy more equities at a time when the market incurred a major collapse. An example follows.

Assume that we begin with $1,000 invested in the Aggressive portfolio. This means that the equity/fixed income allocation is 80 percent/20 percent, or $800 invested in equities and $200 invested in fixed income. Assume that in the first year, equities drop in value by 40 percent while the value of the fixed income portfolio remains unchanged. Our equity portfolio would have decreased by $320 ($800 × 40 percent). Our portfolio would now consist of $480 of equities and $200 of fixed income—a total value of $680. In order to maintain our 80 percent equity allocation, we need to increase our equity position to $544 ($680 × 80 percent). The result is that just when the market has collapsed, we will have to sell $64 of fixed income assets and buy $64 of equities. Alternatively, if additional funds were available, we could

170

purchase an additional $320 of equities, which would return the equity position to $800 and restore the 80/20 mix. It takes a lot of discipline and courage to buy in the face of a market collapse. But this is the only way we could have achieved the superior returns the Aggressive portfolio produced.

Since we know that the Aggressive portfolio produces the higher returns, we begin our stomach acid test here. The investor, keeping in mind Socrates' admonition—Know thyself—must look in the mirror and honestly answer two questions:

- Do I have the courage and discipline to stick with my strategy?

- Will I be able to sleep well if the performance of the single worst year experienced by this portfolio, negative 27 percent (see the Model Portfolio table on page 168), was repeated?

If the answer to both questions is yes, the investor can move on to take the liquidity test. However, the investor *must* answer yes to *both* questions or this portfolio is not the correct one, because he or she may bail out just when it is important to buy. Having sold out at the lows, the investor would almost certainly have been better off with the Defensive portfolio in the first place. In addition, and very important, this poor experience may cause the investor to avoid investing in the equity markets altogether in the future.

If the answers to these questions are no, the investor should move to the left, to the next most aggressive portfolio. The process should then be repeated until an acceptable level of risk is found. Keep in mind that these four portfolios are not the only ones that can be constructed. For example, if our hypothetical investor is not comfortable with the Aggressive portfolio but is willing to accept more risk than is inherent in the Moderate portfolio, a 70 percent equity/30 percent fixed income portfolio could be constructed.

As I have previously mentioned, the investor is making the

choice between sleeping well or eating well. She cannot have it both ways. In other words, an investor choosing the Defensive portfolio must be aware that historically the price for sleeping well (having no loss years and experiencing a standard deviation of less than 6 percent) was leaving more than half of her potential investment dollars on the table ($24.60 versus $11.90).

While there is no one correct choice, it is important to understand the consequences of your choices. Robert Arnott put it this way: "If investors invest in a fashion that exceeds their own risk tolerance, so that when things go awry (as they inevitably will from time to time) they must abandon their strategy, they have done themselves a disservice by engaging in the strategy in the first place."[101] This insight is especially true in light of the recent spectacular performance of the U.S. equity markets, which have experienced the greatest bull run ever without a significant correction.

Unreasonable Expectations

Since there has not been a major downturn since the short-lived but painful crash of 1987, it is estimated that 80 percent of all money now invested by individuals has never experienced a significant bear market that would test their discipline. A lesson particularly relevant to today's market is the reminder that the rewards of investing in equities are compensation for the risks entailed. The understanding of tolerance for and ability to absorb risk, along with the length of your investment time horizon, should play a critical role in your choice of portfolio. The next time you marvel at the returns your portfolio has produced in recent years, remember that those returns were compensation for taking risk—the risk is that you are likely to experience some painful losses in the future. If you are not psychologically prepared or financially able to absorb those painful experiences and to think of bear markets as temporary periods when the market is wearing a big "For Sale" sign, your asset allocation should reflect the appropriate risk tolerance.

The Liquidity Test

Taking the liquidity test determines the amount of liquid assets—which are not at risk—required by the investor to meet near-term cash needs as well as other potential unanticipated requirements. As I have shown, even a highly diversified portfolio of risky equity assets can experience periods of at least three years without positive returns.

The liquidity test begins by determining the amount of cash reserve one may need to meet unanticipated needs for cash such as medical bills, car or home repair, or even the loss of a job. Financial planners generally recommend a cash reserve of about six months of ordinary expenses. If our investor has expenses of $5,000 per month, a cash reserve of $30,000 should be built before making any equity investments. The investor must then determine those cash needs that must be met within the next five years, for example, the purchase of a car, a down payment on a home, or college tuition. Any cash needs that fall within this time frame should be invested in short-term fixed income instruments, the maturity of which should generally be matched to the date of the known cash need.

With any investment portfolio, the risk of the expected outcome not occurring decreases dramatically as the time horizon increases. The longer the time horizon, the more certain the outcome. In fact, once the investment horizon exceeds five years, the likelihood of a negative outcome is sharply reduced. As we saw with our model portfolios covering the past 23 years, portfolios using the principles of Modern Portfolio Theory would not have experienced a negative return in any five-year period. Once an investment exceeds 10 years, history tells us that one is far less likely to experience a negative return even from a portfolio that is not highly diversified. Therefore, I recommend that an investor consider using the following guideline to determine the appropriate fixed income and equity allocation.

Asset Allocation Time Horizon Guideline

Time Horizon	Equity (%)	Fixed Income (%)
5 Years or less	0	100
6 Years	20	80
7 Years	40	60
8 Years	60	40
9 Years	80	20
10 Years or longer	100	0

To look at an example of how this table can be put to work, assume that our hypothetical investor has $250,000 available to invest and the following cash needs: four years of college tuition, room and board at $25,000 a year, beginning in year six; $30,000 for a new car in five; and $30,000 for emergency reserves (6 months × $5,000 per month in living expenses). The investor should hold $60,000 in short-term fixed income investments for a car and for emergency expenses. The amount needed to be held in short-term fixed income investments to meet the college expenses is calculated as follows.

Year 6	$25,000 × 80% = $20,000
Year 7	$25,000 × 60% = $15,000
Year 8	$25,000 × 40% = $10,000
Year 9	$25,000 × 20% = $ 5,000
Total	$50,000

Note that as the time horizon increases (and the risk of an expected outcome not occurring decreases), we reduce the percentage allocated to fixed income assets.

The total allocated to fixed income investments should be $60,000 for the car and an emergency reserve plus $50,000 for college tuition for a total of $110,000. Having $250,000 to invest, the asset allocation to equities should not exceed $140,000, or 56 percent—regardless of the outcome of the stomach acid test. In fact, if the stomach acid test produced a maximum acid level of equities below 56 percent, that lower number should be the upper limit. In other words, the equity asset allocation should always be the lower of the two test outcomes.

Keep in mind that the 5-to-10-year/0–100 percent equity allocation ladder described in this guideline is just a guideline. More aggressive investors, willing to accept more risk, might choose a ladder that covers 3–10 years and add an equity allocation of about 15 percent per annum beginning in year four. It's the discipline of the process, not the formula, that is important. However, I would certainly not recommend making any equity investments with cash needed within a three-year time frame. I would also recommend that any cash that is available for investment for a period exceeding 15 years (preferably 10) should be invested in equities, even for the most conservative of investors.

In addition to insuring that an investor has sufficient funds to meet all his or her known short-term expenses as well as an emergency reserve, the liquidity test provides another benefit. Since an investor will have set aside sufficient funds in a not-at-risk, liquid safety net, he or she should feel secure when the inevitable periods of poor market performance occur. With sufficient funds to cover expenses and a well-diversified portfolio, an investor improves the chances of having the discipline and courage to ride out the inevitable bad years. Difficult periods are built right into our investment strategy.

The Annual Checkup

Our hypothetical investor should repeat the dual test procedure annually, for three reasons:

- His or her personal situation may change, causing a change in tolerance for risk. For example, our investor may have inherited a large sum of money or experienced the loss of a job. It is important to understand that our investor's tolerance for risk should not change because market conditions have changed. If this occurs, the investor did not look in the mirror carefully enough at the outset. Investors must acknowledge the risk they are accepting and be sure they are prepared to have the courage of their convictions.

- His or her investment time horizons may have changed. For example, the expenses originally projected are now one year closer in time and therefore probably require a greater allocation to the fixed income asset class.

- During the year he or she may have accumulated additional cash, which is now available for investment.

Now that you have seen how you can build a tailored portfolio and adapt it to your changing financial circumstances, I'll explain how to make the allocation decisions that relate to tax issues.

Allocating Assets Between Taxable and Nontaxable Accounts

The only thing that hurts more than paying an income tax is not having to pay an income tax. —Lord Thomas R. Duwar

Earlier I discussed the substantial impact that taxes can have on returns. Today, with the popularity of IRAs, 401k's, SEPs, Keoghs, a myriad of other types of deferred compensation plans, variable annuities, and variable life insurance, most investors have some understanding about allocating assets between taxable and tax-deferred accounts. Which asset classes should be in your taxable account, and which should be in your tax-deferred account? Keep in mind that the preferred allocations between taxable and tax-deferred accounts that follow are done on a relative basis. In other words, given the ability to do so, an investor is almost always better off investing in a tax-deferred account. Investors should, in general, fully utilize their ability to place funds into tax-deferred accounts before allocating any assets to taxable accounts.

A strong word of caution: Because there are some complex issues related to tax-deferred accounts, such as IRAs, variable annuities, and variable life insurance policies, I recommend that you seek the assistance of a tax specialist when making decisions about which type of account to place your assets in.

Fixed Income Assets

These assets serve two purposes. First, they are used to generate current income. If you must have access to the income generated by fixed income investments to meet living expenses, the related assets should be in the taxable portion of a portfolio (unless you have reached the age that allows you to withdraw funds from a tax-deferred account without penalty). If your tax bracket is high, then tax-exempt securities should be considered. Tax-exempt securities typically provide a higher after-tax return than taxable securities for those investors whose tax bracket is above 28 percent at the federal level. Tax-exempt securities should never be held in tax-deferred accounts.

The second purpose fixed income assets serve is to reduce risk (they are less volatile than equities) and to provide the benefits of diversification. Since the interest earned on these assets is in the form of ordinary income, which is taxed at the highest rate, the portion of your fixed income allocation that is not needed to generate cash for living expenses should be allocated to your tax-deferred account.

Equities in General

If equities are held long enough to obtain capital gains treatment, they receive favorable tax treatment. Long-term capital gains are currently taxed at a maximum rate of 28 percent. If you were to put equities into a tax-deferred account, when you eventually withdrew funds they would be taxed at the presumably higher ordinary income tax rates. I do not see the benefit of converting income that is taxed at a low rate into income that is taxed at a high rate. Some studies have shown that if the holding period is very long, and if the rate of return differential between fixed income assets and equities is very large, then the time value of compounding those returns on a tax-deferred basis makes equities the better choice for tax-deferred accounts. Given the uncertainty of future tax rates, and future returns, I would still recommend placing the equity portion of the portfolio into a taxable account.

As I have already shown, owning mutual funds will usually

create taxable income from distributions. The distributions result from dividend income and realized capital gains, both short-term (taxed at ordinary income rates) and long-term (taxed at preferential capital gains rates). The more a fund distributes, the greater the tax impact; the more of the distribution that is in the form of ordinary income, the worse the impact. If a fund distributes significant payments, in the form of dividends or short-term capital gains, that fund should be allocated to the tax-deferred portion of the portfolio. Because passively managed asset class funds have low turnover, which results in relatively little payout in the form of long-term capital gains and even less in the form of short-term gains, such funds are very tax efficient; therefore, they should, in general, be held in the taxable portion of the portfolio. On the other hand, actively managed funds, because they are generally very tax inefficient, should probably be held in the tax-deferred portion of the portfolio. The higher the turnover of the fund, the more it belongs in the tax-deferred portfolio. For the remainder of this chapter, it should be assumed that I am discussing only passively managed funds.

Equities: Small-Cap Versus Large-Cap and Value

Companies that fit into the small capitalization asset class generally pay out far less in the form of dividends than those that fit into the large capitalization or value asset classes. Virtually all the expected return from investments in the small-cap asset class are expected to be in the form of long-term capital gains. Small-cap funds should, therefore, be held in the taxable portion of the portfolio. If your large-cap or value funds pay out significant dividend income, then they should be in the tax-deferred portion of the portfolio.

Equities: Domestic Versus International

If an international equity fund pays dividends, then it may be subject to withholding taxes from the country of origin. The amount withheld reduces the amount of dividend the investor actually receives. If the fund is subject to withholding taxes by a foreign government and is in a taxable account, the IRS allows you to claim a deduction in the form of a foreign tax credit on your return. On the other hand, if that same fund were in an account not subject to current income taxes, the foreign tax credit would have no value. The loss of this tax benefit could reduce your returns by about 0.5 percent per annum. The funds that are likely to be subject to foreign tax credits should, therefore, be placed in taxable accounts. These funds are from the asset classes of either international value or international large capitalization. In order of preference, domestic funds that pay dividends should be placed in a tax-sheltered account, while international funds that pay dividends should be placed in a taxable account. Since international small capitalization stocks are unlikely to pay significant dividends, the foreign tax credit issue is less relevant. Therefore, they can be treated the same as domestic small capitalization funds.

REITs

Because this category of assets is likely to generate substantial current income, we want to treat them like our other fixed income assets and place them in our tax-deferred account. However, if we need access to the cash flow that this asset class generates, we would place them in a taxable account. If you have reached the age when you can withdraw funds from a tax-deferred account without penalty, then they can be held in this type of account.

Variable Annuities and Variable Life Insurance

Variable annuities and variable life insurance contracts may be of value as part of an overall investment and estate tax planning strategy. These contracts provide the ability to defer income taxes until funds are withdrawn. They act in a manner similar to an IRA, and asset allocation decisions involving them should be made with that fact in mind. For example, generally, I would want to hold income-producing asset classes in such policies, but not equity mutual funds that are already tax efficient.

A word of caution, however, on these contracts. They may involve very heavy expenses, both inside the policy and in the form of sales commissions. The heavy sales commissions make these contracts very popular among the people who sell these policies— another example of the need to be careful about whose interests are being served when you are dealing with a financial services firm that generates commissions from product sales. Many lawsuits have resulted from abusive sales tactics. Fortunately, low-load, no-load, and low-expense policies are now being made available either directly to the public or through such firms as Charles Schwab, Fidelity, Vanguard, and Providian. Be sure that in your search for tax-efficient vehicles you do not unnecessarily overpay to obtain that particular benefit. Also keep in mind that tax efficiency can be obtained through passive equity asset class mutual funds without the need to purchase an annuity or an insurance policy. The expenses involved in even the low-expense versions of these vehicles may require holding periods of at least 7 to 10 years before the tax deferral benefit begins to outweigh the increased expenses incurred.

T. Rowe Price learned a lesson about how expensive annuities are in an amusing way. When they began selling variable annuities in October 1995, they introduced a software program for investors that included a questionnaire designed to help them decide whether to put money in the hybrid insurance/investment product or instead into a mutual fund. Each time a client inquired about an annuity, he or she was sent the software. After about six months, T. Rowe Price followed up with market research to see why some investors bought annuities and some didn't. The conclusion: the software had done its job too well. It was the number one reason why investors had decided not to buy an annuity. With the facts, and no sales pressure from someone who didn't have their best interests at heart, investors made the intelligent decision.[102]

You now know that if we have the ability to allocate assets between a tax-deferred account and one that is taxable, there are definite choices to be made.

Before I move on to discuss two important additional concepts—rebalancing and style drift—I want to address another significant asset allocation issue: the tendency for many investors to become too conservative in their allocation decisions.

Avoiding Too Conservative an Asset Class Allocation

There is a tide in the affairs of men, when taken at the flood, leads on to fortune. —Shakespeare, *Julius Caesar*, act 4, scene 3

A ship in port is safe, but that's not what ships are built for.
—Grace Murray Hooper, *A Kick in the Seat of the Pants*

For various reasons, including fear and lack of knowledge, many investors allocate too much of their portfolios to low-returning fixed income asset classes. As I have already shown, Modern Portfolio Theory can be employed to substantially reduce the risks of equity investments through the power of broad, global, passive asset class diversification. Even retired individuals, who rely on their portfolios to generate 100 percent of their cash flow needs, can increase their allocations to the higher returning equity asset classes and thereby reduce the risk that inflation will prevent them from maintaining the standard of living to which they have become accustomed. This section will explain how to accomplish this objective.

Before leading his men down into the valley of the Little Big Horn, it is said that General George Armstrong Custer rallied his troops with the cry, "No guts, no glory." With the benefit of hindsight, it is safe to say that, in his hunt for glory, General Custer did not prudently evaluate the risks involved in his venture. Fortunately for investors, in their search for returns, they do not have to take the kind of risks General Custer took. I believe that there is an approach that even the most conservative investors can use to improve their returns, while at the same time reducing the risk that inflation will erode their ability to maintain their lifestyle.

By now I am sure that you are convinced that:

- Markets reward for risk.

- Equities have outperformed bonds over almost every 10-year period.

- Portfolios using Modern Portfolio Theory do even better, and they do so with less volatility.

These days a 65-year-old retiree has an extended life span of about 20 years; the average married 65-year-old couple has an even longer second-to-die life expectancy. Despite these actuarial facts, too many investors, particularly those dependent on interest income to meet cash flow needs, become too conservative in their asset allocation decisions. Perhaps out of fear, they unnecessarily miss out on the rewards of equity investing in their attempt to avoid risk. Since most investors have at least a 10-year time horizon for a portion of their total available investment assets, this "conservative" strategy subjects them to another risk: that inflation will erode their ability to maintain their lifestyle. Investors need to shift their perception of risk from solely the loss of principal to including the erosion of purchasing power while they are still alive.

In the investment field there is an often-used rule of thumb that your equity allocation should be equal to one hundred minus your age; I consider it a far too conservative approach. What follows is an improved method of weighing one's cash flow needs and the risk of equity investing that uses the liquidity and stomach acid tests we discussed earlier but ignores the "one hundred minus your age" rule.

Many investors who rely totally on interest income to meet living expenses believe that their age reduces the likelihood of recovering from a major loss. Their main objective is to reduce the risk of loss of principal. But how wise is it to place most, if not all, of one's portfolio into fixed income assets? Before you conclude that the conservative approach is best, or even the most risk averse, let us explore an alternative investment strategy.

The Income Generation Approach

Assume an investor wants to generate $100,000 in after-tax income and can earn 5 percent on tax-free municipal bonds. In order to generate the desired $100,000, an investor would need to buy $2 million of municipal bonds ($2,000,000 × 5 percent). Using a 10-year investment horizon (remember that equities have outperformed bonds over almost every 10-year period), the investor purchases a bond that matures in 10 years, at which time his principal is returned to him.

Unfortunately, if inflation averages just 3 percent per year, the principal will then be worth less than $1.5 million in real dollars. In other words, the investor will have experienced a 25 percent reduction in real purchasing power. Obviously, a higher inflation rate will further reduce that investor's ability to maintain his or her lifestyle.

The Laddered Portfolio Approach

If our $2 million investor is willing to accept more investment risk, there is an alternative that can offer a far more favorable outcome. Instead of buying one 10-year bond, our investor buys a "strip" of 10 $100,000 zero coupon bonds, one bond maturing in each of the next 10 years. This type of strip is called a laddered portfolio. A zero coupon bond is a bond that is issued at a discount because it pays no current interest. Instead it increases in value each year, by accruing the interest owed until maturity, at which time all the interest is paid out at once. Based on April 1996 market rates, the cost to an investor to purchase a one-year $100,000 zero coupon bond was about $96,000. After one year, he would receive $100,000 back, giving him a return of about 4.2 percent. A two-year zero coupon bond would cost less than a one-year zero coupon bond of the same face amount, because it would accrue interest for two years, returning the $100,000 face amount at maturity. The longer the maturity, the less the initial cost, because more years of interest will be accrued. Zero coupon bonds are used because they insure that an investor will receive the exact dollar amount needed at the end of the time period. We do not have to worry about what rate we will receive when we reinvest interest received from bonds that pay interest on a periodic basis. Again, at April 1996 market rates, a 10-year strip or portfolio cost $761,000. That strip would provide our $2 million investor with a cash flow of $100,000 per year for 10 years. Knowing that equities have outperformed bonds in virtually every 10-year period, the investor would be in position to invest the remaining $1,239,000 in equities.

Example A.
Creating a 10-year Strip of Zero Coupon Municipal Bonds
Designed to Provide $100,000 of Annual Cash Flow;
Total Cost $761,000

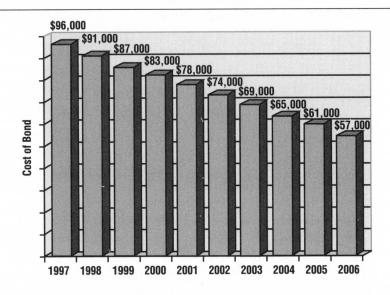

In both scenarios the investor generated the required cash flow of $100,000. In the first case, our investor received $100,000 in interest income each year, and full return of $2 million in principal at the end of the period. In the second case, our investor received the proceeds from the $100,000 zero coupon bond that matured in that particular year. The remaining $1,239,000, was placed in a well-diversified portfolio, such as those used in our earlier models. For the 10- and 20-year periods ending on December 1995, a 100 percent equity model portfolio (we use the 100 percent allocation because we are investing $761,000 in bonds and the remaining balance in equities) would have produced returns of over 15 percent and 19 percent, respectively. Assume, however, that going forward, this type of portfolio would only grow at a compound annual rate of 10 percent per annum. At this rate the original $1,239,000

186

would increase to over $3.2 million, or about 60 percent more than the maturing $2 million bond (see example B). A reasonable assumption of a 12 percent return would result in an ending portfolio balance of $3.8 million. A 15 percent and a 19 percent rate of return would result in portfolios of about $5 and $7 million, respectively. This process definitely improves returns, with an acceptable level of risk, at least in historical terms. At a minimum, the risk/reward ratio is very good. In order to leave the investor with the same $2 million in principal as the bondholder had at the end of the 10-year period, the equity portfolio would have needed to increase at only a 5 percent compound annual rate, before considering taxes. Moreover, the equity portfolio provided much more inflation protection. As noted earlier, equities have consistently provided real, after-inflation rates of returns of 6–7 percent per annum, given a long enough investment time horizon. And 10 years should be long enough. So I ask again, How wise is the conservative investor whose sole investment strategy is to protect his investments against the loss of principal?

Example B.

Growth of $1,239,000 Equity Portfolio at 10 percent per Annum

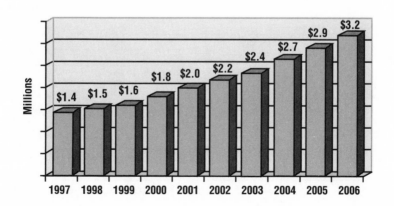

If our investor was so conservative (this is where the stomach acid test comes in) that a 10-year horizon was too short, then a similar portfolio could have been structured over a 15-year time horizon. Keep in mind that equities have outperformed bonds over every 15-year period during the last 70 years. By extending the strip out to 15 years (see example C), our investor would still have $1,014,000 left to invest in equities. At a 10 percent compounded rate of return, this portfolio would have grown to over $4.2 million over 15 years (see example D).

As the examples show, our "conservative" investor might have slept better (assuming he or she wasn't worrying about inflation eating into his or her standard of living). But the investor who chose the alternative of the blended portfolio certainly was eating better and, perhaps, sleeping better too. Remember the lesson explained earlier in this book: Time works in your favor when holding a balanced portfolio, while it works against you when holding a "conservative" 100 percent fixed income portfolio.

Example C.
Creating a 15-year Strip of Zero Coupon Municipal Bonds
Designed to Provide $100,000 of Annual Cash Flow;
Total Cost $986,000

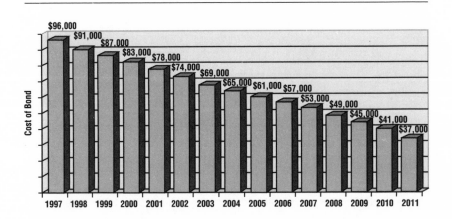

Example D.
Growth of $1,014,000 Equity Portfolio at 10 percent per Annum

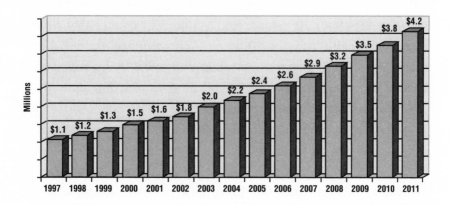

Finally, let me show how even the most conservative $2 million investor can do a better job of making asset allocation decisions. Take the example of a recently retired 65-year-old executive, having the same $100,000 per annum cash need and a 20-year life expectancy. The executive could purchase a strip of bonds out to 20 years at a cost of about $1.1 million. Having provided, with certainty, for her anticipated cash flow needs over the next 20 years, she can "safely" invest the remaining $900,000 in equities. If such a portfolio earned a 10 percent compound rate of return, she would have over $6 million at the end of the period. That is three times the $2 million that would have remained if it had been invested solely in bonds. The resulting portfolio would be available to help maintain the lifestyle to which our executive had become accustomed, should she live beyond her life expectancy. A significant number of such investors will, in fact, live beyond their life expectancies.

Remember that equities are risky only if your investment horizon is short. Consider the following evidence. For a one-year holding period, there is a 5 percent chance that the stock market will fall at least 25 percent and a 5 percent chance that it will rise more than 40 percent. On the other hand, over 30 years there is only a 5 percent chance that a 100 percent stock portfolio will grow by less than 20 percent and a 5 percent chance that it will increase in value by over 50 times. As one increases the investment horizon, the disparity between returns on "risky" equity investments and "conservative" fixed income instruments widens dramatically. Over 20 years, there is only a 5 percent chance that a fixed income portfolio will more than quadruple, while there is a 50 percent chance that an equity portfolio will grow at least eightfold.[103] With a long-term horizon, bonds or any other fixed income investment become the risky investment, because equities provide protection against the erosion of purchasing power by inflation.

Maintaining Your Purchasing Power

The erosion of purchasing power is a very important concern because it affects an investor's ability to maintain his lifestyle. Whether calculating the size of a fixed income portfolio large enough to provide interest income to meet one's needs or constructing a laddered portfolio that will provide the cash flow to meet the same needs, an investor should build into his calculations some reasonable estimate of inflation.

Let's go back to our first example of the investor wanting to generate $100,000 per annum. Actually, he should look to generate $100,000 in the first year, $105,000 in the second year, $110,000 in the third year, and so on. Assuming that he did not underestimate the rate of inflation, the $110,000 generated in the third year will have as much purchasing power as the $100,000 in the first year. In our earlier examples, I did not include the need for a rising income stream because I did not want to complicate an already complex issue. An investor, however, must include an inflation estimate in constructing the laddered portfolio. Given the complexity of each individual's unique situation, it might be prudent to seek the counsel of a financial advisor before proceeding on your own.

Now let's turn to two other very important concepts: portfolio rebalancing and style drift.

CHAPTER 9

♦

Rebalancing and Style Drift

Everything should be made as simple as possible, but not simpler.
                                        —Albert Einstein

My wife is a passionate gardener. She tends her garden with great care and discipline. Each season brings with it the need for certain tasks; if she does not accomplish these tasks, her garden might be filled with weeds, her plants destroyed by bugs, and her trees decayed by disease. The garden must undergo regular maintenance, or it will not produce the desired result. The same regular maintenance must be performed on an investment portfolio, or it is unlikely to produce the expected outcome. One of the most important items on the portfolio maintenance agenda is rebalancing.

Rebalancing a portfolio—the process of restoring a portfolio to its original asset allocations and risk profile—is integral to the winning investment strategy. As was shown in the previous chapter, it is important for every investor to choose the portfolio and asset allocation that meet his or her individual tolerance for risk and are consistent with his or her investment time horizon. Once the original investment allocations have been implemented, the

193

process has only just begun. There are two major reasons why rebalancing is an ongoing process. First, as already discussed, an annual checkup is needed to respond to changes in personal or financial circumstances, as well as the inevitable change in investment time horizons. Second, each asset class within the portfolio is likely to change in value by a different amount during any discrete time period, and this performance variance will affect the amount of risk in the portfolio.

A simple example will illustrate this point. Assume that an investor starting out with $100,000 to invest chooses an asset allocation of 80 percent equities ($80,000) and 20 percent fixed income ($20,000). If the value of the equity portion of the portfolio increases 40 percent while the fixed income portion increases 5 percent, the investor would then have $112,000 in equities and $21,000 in fixed income assets—a total portfolio worth $133,000. The difference in performance of the two asset classes causes the asset allocation to change from 80 percent/20 percent to 84 percent/16 percent. The portfolio now has different risk and return characteristics than the original portfolio; its expected return is greater, but so is its risk.

	Original Portfolio		New Portfolio	
Equity allocation	80%	$80,000	84%	$112,000
Fixed income allocation	20%	$20,000	16%	$21,000
Total portfolio	100%	$100,000	100%	$133,000

Two methods may be used to rebalance the portfolio and restore the desired 80/20 asset allocation. The first is to simply reallocate. A portfolio of $133,000 with an 80 percent/20 percent asset allocation would have $106,400 in equities and $26,600 in fixed income assets. The investor would have to sell $5,600 of equities and buy an equal amount of fixed income assets to restore the portfolio to the original level of risk. Unfortunately, this method of rebalancing incurs transaction fees. And, unless the rebalancing occurs in a nontaxable account, taxes will be due on the capital gain realized on the sale of $5,600 of equities. Fortunately, the impact will not be great because we only sold a small portion of the equity portfolio. Taxes, however, should be avoided, or deferred, whenever possible because they reduce long-term returns. Therefore, an investor must exercise judgment when weighing the benefits of rebalancing against the taxes generated. If taxes are not an issue, as with a tax-deferred account such as an IRA, there is no reason not to undertake regular rebalancing.

There is a more tax-friendly way of rebalancing a portfolio. If an investor has generated additional investable funds, they can be used to add to the fixed income portion of the portfolio so as to restore the original 80 percent/20 percent ratio. With a current equity portfolio of $112,000, one would need a total portfolio of $140,000 ($112,000 ÷ 80 percent = $140,000) to restore one's desired allocation. With one's portfolio currently valued at $133,000, one would need to purchase $7,000 of fixed income assets to rebalance the portfolio. By adding new funds, one avoids the taxable event, and because there are fewer trades, transaction costs are reduced. If there is insufficient new cash to fully accomplish the desired rebalancing, a combination of the two strategies can be used.

	End of Period Portfolio		Rebalanced Portfolio	
Equity allocation	84%	$112,000	80%	$112,000
Fixed income allocation	16%	$21,000	20%	$28,000
Total portfolio	100%	$133,000	$100%	$140,000

Style Drift

In addition to being a passionate gardener, my wife is an excellent cook. However, she always runs into problems when trying to get a recipe from her mom, who measures ingredients not by teaspoons or tablespoons but by "a little bit of this" or "a pinch of that." My wife does her best to interpret this folk wisdom, but her dishes never taste quite the same as my mother-in-law's. For example, if you deviate from a recipe by adding oregano when salt is called for, your result will drift away from what the original recipe produced. While the risks are usually low when you change a cooking recipe, changing an investment strategy can be a recipe for disaster. For example, when the manager of the domestic mutual fund you own decides to ad lib and buy some shares of Mexican companies, this manager is subjecting you to what is known as style drift. Instead of merely having a dish that tastes funny, you will own a portfolio that varies from the risk profile you expected and were willing to accept.

Rebalancing a portfolio restores the investor's original recipe: his or her desired risk profile. Without regularly rebalancing a portfolio, an investor will find that style drift has crept in. If the investor in our example had not rebalanced his portfolio, it would have drifted, unintentionally, toward a more aggressive style. I have shown how important it is to choose the portfolio allocation that is appropriate for each investor. Not only should you not allow market movements to change your asset allocation and undermine your chosen strategy, but you should not allow active portfolio managers to subject your portfolio to style drift.

The charters of most actively managed mutual funds give their portfolio managers great freedom to shift their allocations between asset classes at their discretion. Investors in such funds not only lose control of their asset allocation decisions, but they also end up taking unintended risks by unknowingly investing in markets, or types of instruments, they wanted to avoid. Fidelity Magellan investors learned this lesson the hard way.

Over the years, many investors have placed the equity portion of their portfolio in the world's largest mutual fund, Fidelity's Magellan. Unfortunately, in February 1996 Magellan's asset allocation was only 70 percent equity; 20 percent was in bonds, and 10 percent was in short-term marketable securities. Magellan's investment manager at the time, the highly regarded Jeffrey Vinik, was obviously making a big bet that long-term bonds and short-term marketable securities would outperform the equity markets. How did his bet affect the investor's asset allocations? Again, assume that our investor with $100,000 to invest seeks an 80 percent equity/20 percent fixed income allocation. She invests her entire $80,000 equity allocation in Fidelity Magellan; due to the strategy deployed by Mr. Vinik, she actually had only $56,000 ($80,000 × 70 percent) invested in equities.

	Desired Allocation		*Actual Allocation*	
Equity allocation	80%	$80,000	56%	$56,000
Fixed income allocation	20%	$20,000	44%	$44,000
Total portfolio	100%	$100,000	100%	$100,000

Our investor's equity allocation was subjected to style drift, in that her exposure to the equity markets, at 56 percent, was less than the desired 80 percent. By placing funds with an active manager she allowed someone else to modify her strategy. The key issue is not the outcome of Mr. Vinik's decision but the investor's loss of control of the asset allocation process. Incidentally, the market subsequently soared to new highs, bonds fell in value, and Mr. Vinik moved on "to pursue other career alternatives." Notably, for the period February 1985 to June 1995, the composition of Fidelity's Magellan fund "varied over time to such a degree that it would have been virtually impossible for investors to determine the asset classes in which they were investing, or the risks to which they were being exposed."[104]

The poor performance over the past few years of the industry's largest and arguably one of its most successful funds has created problems for advocates of active management. John Rekenthaler, the editor at Morningstar, admitted:

> I have argued for years that Magellan was not only wonderful for Fidelity, but also for active managers in the fund industry. Magellan's record argued that fund managers could outperform the market. But Magellan's trouble . . . is one more chip away at active management. If Magellan can be mortal, then all these funds are mortal, giving more credence to the concept of investing in passive index funds which try to match market benchmarks such as the S & P 500 rather than beat them.[105]

This admission is all the more remarkable considering that it comes from a service that provides ratings on mutual funds.

If you think what happened to investors in Fidelity's Magellan Fund is an isolated incident, think again. The Strong Discovery Fund was a top performer from its inception in 1987 through 1995. However, through September 1996, while the S & P 500 was up 5 percent, investors in Strong Discovery experienced a loss of over 10 percent. The active manager of this fund managed to underperform the market by over 15 percent because he bet investors' money on a market downturn. Like Magellan's Vinik, he shifted fund assets from equities to the bond market. Unlike Vinik, he made a further bet on a market correction; by shorting the S & P 500 Index through the use of futures contracts, he bet that he could buy back the contracts he had shorted at a lower price, at a later date. (This sell high, buy low strategy is a reverse version of what investors probably thought he was being paid to do—buy low and sell high.) Unfortunately for the fund's investors, the market correction did not come. By midyear he threw in the towel on this strategy, and he loaded up on equities just as the market began a negative correction. The good news for him was that, since his name is Richard Strong, he didn't have to worry about being fired. Unfortunately, there was no such good news for the investors in his fund. While they had relied on this fund for the equity portion of their portfolio, they instead ended up with a big bond position and a big derivative position (the S & P 500 futures contracts). In other words, like the investors in the Fidelity Magellan Fund, they lost control of the risks they wanted to take.[106]

You should also know that just one year earlier the Strong Discovery Fund had carried Morningstar's coveted five-star rating. So much for relying on ratings. Rating services like Morningstar and the trade publications that cover the financial markets have a perfect track record of predicting the past, but they have not demonstrated an ability to consistently predict the future. As a demonstration of their ability to predict the past, Morningstar subsequently downgraded the Strong Discovery Fund to two-star status.

Investors in passive asset class funds are not subject to style drift, because passive asset class funds buy and hold assets within only their specific asset class. On the other hand, very few active managers stick to their knitting. Domestic funds often hold foreign securities. Small-cap funds often hold mid- to small-cap stocks. Value funds hold growth stocks. And most active managers raise or lower their equity allocation based on their feel for the market. Now is an appropriate time to remember the lesson you learned about the three-factor model at the end of chapter 5. The three-factor model teaches that portfolio returns are determined by the amount of exposure investors have to each of the discrete risk factors—equities, size, and value. I have already given evidence of how style-drifting active managers prevent investors from controlling this all-important determinant of returns. Here's some additional evidence.

The Center for Research in Security Pricing (CRSP) at the University of Chicago defines small-cap stocks as stocks that fall within deciles 9–10; they are the ones that return the largest size premiums. The ninth decile of stocks includes those with a market capitalization of about $200 million and under. The tenth decile of stocks includes those with a market capitalization of about $100 million and under. Investors desiring exposure to this asset class can accomplish this objective by purchasing a small-cap mutual fund. Or can they? According to the Morningstar database, as of October 1996, there were over 120 actively managed mutual funds that Morningstar classified as small-cap funds despite the fact that the average market capitalization of the stocks within them was over $500 million. There were also 15 funds that Morningstar classified as small-cap funds that had average market caps of over $800 million. There were six funds that Morningstar classified as small-cap funds that had market caps of over $900 million. A market cap of $900 million would place a company well into the upper half of all companies ranked by market size. Investors in any one of these six "small-cap" funds certainly weren't exposed to the small-cap risk factor that they were seeking. Of all the funds that Morningstar profiles in its small company category, only 11 would qualify as small-cap funds under the CRSP definition.

Investors who want exposure to the small-cap risk factor should:

- Seek a fund that has an average market cap of $100 to $150 million, or less.

- Invest in only a passively managed small-cap fund.

Since the charters of actively managed mutual funds give their managers considerable latitude to create style drift, asset class "name tags" like Morningstar's are of no substantive value to investors. Only pure passively managed asset class funds enable investors to achieve the asset allocation and risk exposure they desire.

Clearly, in addition to poor performance and tax inefficiency, active managers create unintended risks for investors and cause them to lose exposure to their desired risk factors. The obvious question: Do actively managed mutual funds provide entertainment value that is significant enough to compensate for all the negative attributes?

Rebalancing—Buy Low and Sell High

In addition to providing the all-important benefit of avoiding style drift, rebalancing can also add to portfolio returns. The rebalancing process is quite simple. It allows the investor to reduce the size of his position in the asset classes that performed relatively the best in the period (selling high), and increase the position in the asset classes that performed relatively the worst in the same period (buying low). Isn't it every investor's dream to buy low and sell high? This process has been shown to add 1–2 percent per annum to returns. And the more volatile the asset classes are within the portfolio, the greater the effect of the rebalancing, because you are buying at lower lows and selling at higher highs.

The rebalancing process is one of the reasons the model portfolios in our examples outperformed the market. The following analogy may help to clarify the situation. Asset classes do not go up or down in a straight line any more than .300 hitters get 3 hits in every 10 at bats. A .300 batter who goes 2 for 20 (.100) will all of a sudden go 13 for 30 (.433) and bat .300 for the entire period.

Like good hitters who over a season or their career will bat .300, asset classes provide predictable returns over the long term—and the longer the time frame, the more predictable the returns. The problem for investors is that just as one cannot predict when a hitter will either go into a slump or go on a hot streak, one cannot predict when any particular asset class will be a winner or loser. The good news is that investors don't need that particular skill to be successful. All they need do is regularly rebalance and have faith that markets work in the long run.

The most dramatic impact of the combined benefits of diversification and rebalancing is illustrated by a simulation of returns, performed by DFA, of an emerging market asset class strategy for the period 1988–1995. The simulation covered the countries Argentina, Brazil, Indonesia, Malaysia, Mexico, Portugal, Thailand, and Turkey. While the average return for the eight emerging market countries was 18.14 percent per annum, an investor who rebalanced annually (so that at the beginning of each year each country would represent one-eighth of the portfolio) would have seen her return increase to 29.72 percent per annum. The benefit of diversification and annual rebalancing was an impressive increase in return of 11.58 percent per annum. Had she rebalanced monthly, the return would have improved to 31.57 percent per annum, providing incremental returns of 13.43 percent per annum. (See exhibit C.) The reason the benefit of diversification was so dramatic was that she was investing in a highly volatile asset class. As noted earlier, the more volatile the portfolio, the greater the benefit of rebalancing. Investors should not normally expect an 11 percent or a 14 percent benefit from rebalancing. Nevertheless, it is a very valuable tool, which not only maintains your risk profile but also enhances returns. It is important to note that the more volatile, or risky, the portfolio, the more important it is to rebalance on a regular basis.

Adding Discipline to the Process

Increased returns are not the only benefit of rebalancing; it also provides discipline to the investment process. Rebalancing provides investors with practice for resisting the temptation to second-guess their strategy during the inevitable difficult periods. The time to be a buyer, instead of a panicked seller, is when an asset class is performing poorly. Rebalancing in good times, when markets are rising, enables you to develop the skills and the discipline to do it in tough times. I think it is easier for most investors to sell and take a profit than to buy when the market has just moved sharply lower.

Rebalancing should be performed as part of the annual portfolio checkup. It should also be done whenever new funds are available for investment. For example, when a mutual fund makes a year-end distribution, instead of automatically reinvesting the distribution in the same fund, redirect the distribution to other asset classes in order to accomplish as much rebalancing as possible. Finally, rebalancing should be done whenever the markets have undergone significant moves that have caused your asset allocation to get out of alignment.

The 5 percent/25 percent Rule

Rebalancing generally incurs transaction fees, and it may have tax implications. Therefore, it should only be done either when new funds are available for investment or when your asset allocation has shifted substantially out of alignment. I suggest using a 5 percent/25 percent rule: Rebalancing should only occur if the change in an asset class's allocation is greater than either an absolute 5 percent or 25 percent of the original percentage allocation.

203

For example, if an asset class was given an allocation of *10 percent*, applying the 5 percent rule, one would not rebalance unless that asset class's allocation had either risen to 15 percent (*10 percent* + 5 percent) or fallen to 5 percent (*10 percent* − 5 percent). Using the 25 percent rule one would, however, reallocate if it had risen or fallen by just 2.5 percent (*10 percent* × 25 percent) to either 12.5 percent (*10 percent* + 2.5 percent) or 7.5 percent (*10 percent* − 2.5 percent). In this case, the 25 percent figure was the governing factor. If one had a 50 percent asset class allocation, the 5 percent/25 percent rule would cause the 5 percent figure to be the governing factor, since 5 percent is less than 25 percent of 50 percent, which is 12.5 percent. In other words, one rebalances if either the 5 percent or the 25 percent test indicates the need to do so.

The portfolio should undergo the 5 percent/25 percent test on a quarterly basis, and the test should be applied at three levels:

- At the broad level of equities and fixed income;

- At the level of domestic and international asset classes;

- At the more narrowly defined individual asset class level (such as emerging markets, real estate, small-cap, value, and so on).

For example, suppose one had 10 equity asset classes, each with an allocation of 6 percent, resulting in an equity allocation of 60 percent. If each equity class appreciated so that it then constituted 11 percent of the portfolio, no rebalancing would be required if one only looked at the individual asset class level (the 5 percent/25 percent rule was not triggered). However, looking at the broader equity class level, one sees that rebalancing is required. With 10 equity asset classes each constituting 11 percent of the portfolio, the equity asset class as a whole is now at 66 percent. The equity allocation increasing from 60 percent to 66 percent would trigger the 5 percent/25 percent rule. The reverse situation may occur, where the broad asset classes remain within guidelines but the individual classes do not. Once again, the 5 percent/25 percent test is just a guideline. You can create your own guideline for rebalancing for risk. The discipline that the process provides is far more important than the ratios used.

In summary, rebalancing offers many advantages and is an important part of the investment process.

- It should be performed regularly, using a disciplined approach, such as the 5 percent/25 percent rule.

- It should be done whenever new investment dollars are available.

- It adds discipline to the investment process and maintains control of the most important investment decision, asset allocation.

- It allows investors to avoid style drift.

- It improves returns.

And remember: Active management inevitably causes investors to lose control of the asset allocation process and to experience style drift without the ability to rebalance.

CHAPTER 10

◆

Implementing the Winning Strategy

The beginning is the most important part of the work.
—Plato, *Republic*

It is now time to put to work everything you know about Modern Portfolio Theory and passive asset class investing. The implementation of this strategy begins with the creation of an investment policy statement. This chapter will focus on providing you with the information you need to develop your own investment policy statement, as well as the skills to implement that policy. I will also discuss the merits of using a financial advisor. For those investors not comfortable enough to go it alone, a checklist is provided to help you with selecting such an advisor.

The Investment Policy Statement: 11 Easy Steps Toward a Positive Investment Experience

*I do not believe in a fate that falls on men however they act;
but I do believe in a fate that falls on them unless they act.*
—Gilbert K. Chesterton

*In investment management, the real opportunity to achieve
superior results is not in scrambling to outperform the market,
but in establishing and adhering to appropriate investment
policies over the long term—policies that position the portfolio
to benefit from riding the main long-term forces of the market.*
—Charles Ellis, *Investment Policy*

In the course of my career, I have operated several businesses and served as a consultant to many others. From these experiences I discovered that an important ingredient of success is to put a business plan in place before the start of operations. A business plan serves as a guidepost and provides the discipline needed to adhere to a strategy over time. Of course, as with any plan, a business plan must be reviewed on a regular basis in order to adapt to changing market conditions. Since serious investors should manage their assets as a business, the development of a business plan—or, in this case, an investment policy statement (and an annual review of that statement)—is a critical step toward improving the likelihood of success of that plan.

Support for investment policy statements comes from Meir Statman, a behavioral economist at Santa Clara University. "Our psyches hold the key to much of our investment behavior." He likens the situation to antilock brakes. "When at high speed, the car in front of us stops quickly, we instinctively hit the brake pedal hard and lock 'em up. It doesn't matter that all the studies show that when the brakes lock, we lose control." Statman suggests that investors need antilock brakes for their investment portfolios as well.

> Instinctively we react to investment situations in ways that might have saved our lives fighting on distant battlefields long ago. But, today they are counterproductive, like locking up our brakes. When the market drops, our instinctive fear to flight is so strong, even the most rational investors find themselves caving in, to their own demise. And market tops can often be called soon after the staunchest of bears throws in the towel and turns bullish.[107]

An investment policy statement can act as an investor's antilock braking system.

In short, your own investment policy statement will provide you with the discipline to stick with your plan and will remove the emotion from the investment decision process.

Before writing an investment policy statement, you should thoroughly review your financial and personal status. The financial situation, tolerance for risk, need for emergency reserves, and investment time horizon not only varies from investor to investor but changes over time for each individual. To properly develop a formal investment policy statement, I recommend that you begin by listing all your financial assets and liabilities. Once this is complete, you should take the following steps:

Step 1. Take the liquidity test, insuring that a cash reserve is created first. An amount equal to six months' normal spending should be held in liquid assets such as a money market account or other forms of short-term fixed income assets.

Step 2. Continuing the liquidity test, construct a ladder projecting your forecasted cash needs out to 10 years. Include such items as a down payment on a home, college tuition payments, and so on. Then apply the formula provided in chapter 8 for the liquidity test.

This formula will give you the minimum amount that you should allocate to fixed income assets.

Step 3. Take the stomach acid test, using the model portfolios from chapter 8. Make sure that you are willing and able to stick with your model portfolio through the inevitable bad days. Remember to choose the portfolio furthest to the right (the most aggressive) that still enables you to pass the stomach acid test.

Step 4. Compare the results of the stomach acid test and the liquidity test and choose the one that has the higher (more conservative) fixed income allocation.

Step 5. Compare the allocation determined in step 4 with the allocation that would be derived from the discussion in chapter 8 on avoiding too conservative an asset allocation. If the fixed income allocation produced by the laddered approach is higher (more conservative) than that produced by step 4, proceed with the allocation from step 4. *However, if the laddered portfolio approach produces a lower (more aggressive) fixed income allocation than does step 4, I recommend that you strongly reconsider the conclusion you reached in step 4. You should consider the allocation derived from the laddered portfolio approach.* Remember, the more conservative or nervous you are, the longer your investment ladder can be. A conservative investor might build a laddered portfolio out to 10 years. A more conservative investor might go out to 15 years, and the most conservative could go out to 20 years.

Setting Investment Objectives

Once these initial five steps are completed, you are ready to write the first part of your investment policy statement: your investment strategy objectives. This part of the process is very important, because it forces you to perform a sanity check on your asset allocation decision. To illustrate, let me share the experience of Philip, a good friend and client of my firm.

Philip is an extremely nervous investor. His stomach acid test would probably produce an equity allocation that would asymptotically approach zero. He knows, however, that a very low equity allocation is apt to produce very little, if any, growth in the real value of his portfolio, which would be in direct conflict with his personal objective, which is to retire within 10 to 15 years. To attain his objective, Philip knows that he must take more risk. Having studied the model portfolios, he concludes that in order to retire within his desired time frame he must choose an equity allocation of at least 80 percent. The lower the equity allocation, the longer he would have to continue in the workforce. The results of the stomach acid test proved to be in direct conflict with his personal goals. I told Philip that there was no correct answer to this conundrum. He would have to choose which one of his objectives would have the greater priority, the need to sleep well or his desire for early retirement. Ultimately, Philip decided that his early retirement objective should take priority. He realized that this decision was apt to produce many sleepless nights and that his ability and willingness to stay the course might be sorely tested; accordingly, he immediately purchased a 10-year supply of Extra-Strength Maalox.

Philip's case perfectly illustrates why a written investment policy is necessary. Having written and signed his investment policy statement, Philip had carefully thought through the process; he understood the risks and anticipated the inevitable bad days. He was now more likely to stick with his investment strategy than he otherwise would have been.

Step 6. Write down the goals that you have set for your investment portfolio.

Step 7. Check to see if your goals are in conflict with the results of the first five steps. If not, continue to step 8. Otherwise, you will have to decide whether sleeping well has priority over eating well.

Step 8. Specifically list the percentage of assets you wish to allocate to equities and debt. This step is important, as it will provide discipline to the rebalancing process discussed in chapter 9. Then, within those two broad categories, establish the appropriate percentage allocations for each of the individual asset classes (such as small-cap, value, U. S., international, emerging markets, and so on). Next list the ranges within which you will allow market movements to cause the designated allocation to drift before you will rebalance your portfolio. In chapter 9 a 5 percent/25 percent guideline was suggested.

The range you would be willing to tolerate at the broad asset class level might be:

	Minimum	Target	Maximum
Equity:	55%	60%	65%
Fixed income:	35%	40%	45%

The range you would be willing to tolerate at the individual asset class level might be: minimum 7.5 percent; target 10 percent; maximum 12.5 percent.

Since rebalancing may generate capital gains taxes, whenever possible rebalance with new investment dollars or do so using tax-advantaged accounts.

Step 9. Determine the investment style that must be used if a mutual fund is to be included in your portfolio. You may decide that all funds should be passively managed. If you seek excitement, you may decide to allocate a small percentage, perhaps 5 percent of your portfolio, to individual stocks or to actively managed funds (your entertainment portfolio). If you do include individual stocks in your portfolio, remember to include them in the asset allocation within which they fall (such as U. S. small-cap).

Now you must establish procedures and controls to make sure your portfolio is being properly monitored and adapted, when necessary, to any changing personal situations. Establishing such controls and procedures is especially important if you have engaged an investment advisory firm to assist you in the investment process.

Step 10. A periodic schedule of events and reviews should be established:

Monthly: Review each monthly statement from the custodian holding your assets to be certain that it includes all current holdings and any transactions that occurred during the preceding month.

Quarterly: Review your portfolio thoroughly to see if rebalancing is required. If you have engaged a financial advisor, he or she should be responsible for scheduling the meeting and setting the agenda and the objectives of that meeting. Prior to the meeting the advisor should prepare and send to you a report showing the current allocations, so that you are both prepared to analyze your portfolio in depth. At this meeting there should also be a brief review of your investment policy statement to determine whether it requires alteration.

Annually: There should be a thorough review of your portfolio, including rebalancing, especially if your investment time horizon has changed over the year. A change in investment time horizon will probably change the results of the liquidity test and may require that you alter your asset allocations. Because of certain events, it may also be necessary to change your established risk profile to one that is either more aggressive or more conservative. There should also be a thorough review of your investment policy statement to determine whether any alterations need to be made, perhaps because unanticipated academic research has uncovered superior strategies. Finally, there should be an estate and tax planning review to either make any required changes or to take advantage of emerging opportunities.

It is absolutely necessary for you to take control and fully implement your investment policy statement. More than anything else, the implementation of your statement will determine the performance of your portfolio. Even if you engage a financial advisor, make sure that it is you who ultimately determines the contents of your investment policy statement. Remember that it is your statement, not your advisor's. He or she should merely provide information and serve as devil's advocate, making sure that you have asked the right questions and have thought through the consequences of your answers. Your advisor may even make recommendations, it being understood that the consequences (risk and return implications) of those recommendations are fully explained. Since your ability and willingness to handle risk is best known to you, final investment decisions should never be delegated.

Step 11. You and your financial advisor, if one has been engaged, should sign the investment policy statement. This action considerably heightens your commitment to carry out your investment plan. This is important because, as Johann Wolfgang von Goethe said, "To think is easy. To act is difficult. To act as one thinks is the most difficult of all." Finally, by having both parties sign the document, you minimize any confusion over objectives, policies, procedures, and appropriate investments. The dual signature also serves to protect each party in the event of a future disagreement.

Before concluding this discussion, I need to explain why a very important, possibly even the most important part, of any investment policy statement is a commitment to save and invest as much as possible, as early in life as possible.

A Penny Saved, a Fortune Earned

Time and tide wait for no man. —Traditional saying

Archimedes, a great mathematician of ancient Greece, believed that the most powerful force in the world was the lever. "Give me one long enough and I could lift the world itself." If Archimedes had understood the power of compound interest, he might have thought that compound interest is the most powerful force. Benjamin Franklin called it the "eighth wonder of the world."

When facing the choice between investing or consuming, investors need to have a better understanding of compound interest. Because of the power of compound interest, investors should start saving and investing at as early an age as possible. This advice is at least as important as any provided in this book. The following is a dramatic example of why this is true.

Sally begins to save $5,000 a year at age 25. She continues to save this amount for 10 years, until age 34, and then stops saving. Sam, on the other hand, does not start saving until age 35. He then saves $5,000 a year for the next 30 years. Sally will have saved a total of $50,000 ($5,000 × 10). Sam will have saved a total of $150,000 ($5,000 × 30), or three times as much. Both investors placed their savings in investment accounts that generated the same 10 percent rate of return on their investment.

By age 65, Sally will have generated a portfolio of about $1.4 million. Despite his having saved and invested three times as many dollars, Sam's portfolio will have grown to only about $820,000, 40 percent less than Sally's. At age 75, the two portfolios will have grown to $3.6 million and $2.2 million, respectively.

Let's see what happens if an investor defers saving for an even longer period. Jane begins to save at age 45. Having waited until age 45 to begin saving, and investing, she must save $24,000 per

Total Amount Invested

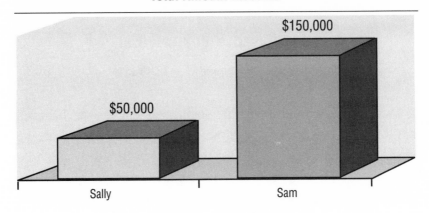

Portfolio at Age 65

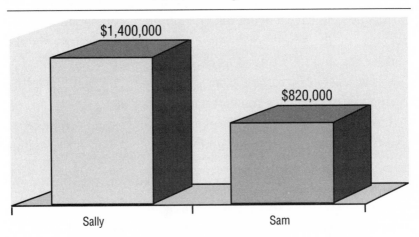

Portfolio at Age 75

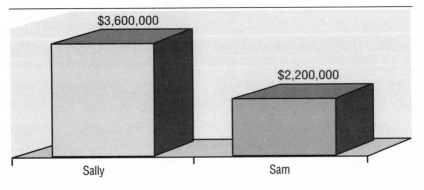

annum for the next 20 years to achieve the same portfolio as Sally, who had saved only $5,000 per annum for 10 years. John defers his savings program even longer and begins to save at age 55. He must save $87,000 per year for the next 10 years to achieve the same portfolio as Sally.

Amount Saved per Year

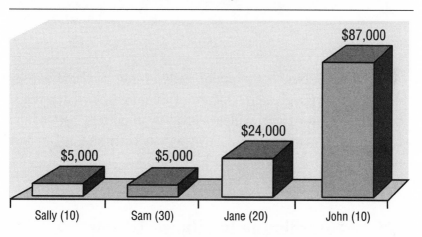

Total Amount Invested

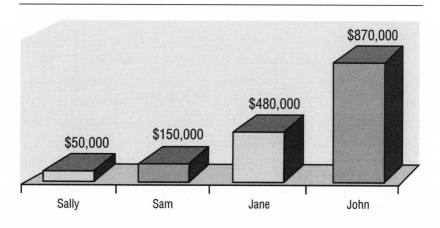

Portfolio at Age 65

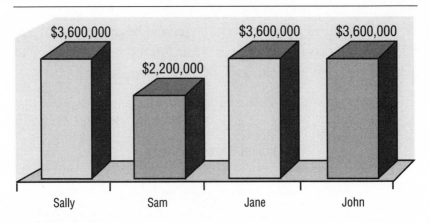

By deferring some consumption early in life, investors will be able to enjoy a far greater standard of living in their later years. The examples are clear evidence that an important part of the winning investment strategy is investing as early and as often as possible.

Selecting an Investment Advisor

If you don't know where you are going you will probably end up someplace else. —Laurence J. Peter

You now have the knowledge and tools to successfully implement the winner's strategy using passive asset class investing. However, even though you have the necessary information to do so, you may not be comfortable enough to go it alone; so you may decide to utilize the services of a financial advisor to help with the process. Even if you are comfortable enough with your knowledge of the financial markets to go it alone, there are a variety of reasons to hire a financial advisor.

Tennis players know that a pro can teach them the skills needed to make the variety of shots required for a well-rounded game. The pro can also provide the winning strategy and the discipline to stick with that strategy. That is why even the top players in the world continue to have a coach. Investors can benefit from "coaching" in the same way a tennis player does. Just like the tennis pro, a good financial advisor will provide:

- The education necessary for the investor to play the game.

- The winning strategy.

- The discipline to stick with that strategy.

This last point is particularly important in light of the evidence provided by two studies. The first, Mark Carhart's study, the most comprehensive ever done on mutual fund performance, found that since 1962 the average no-load fund outperformed the average load fund by 0.6 percent per annum. And that did not even take into account the commissions load fund investors pay. The second study, by Dalbar Financial Services, a Boston-based consulting firm, found that the actual returns earned by investors in no-load funds was 1.2 percent *less* than the return earned by investors in load funds. How could that possibly be? The answer is that the load investor, having paid a sales charge, was less likely to attempt market timing or to engage in performance chasing: 1.8 percent (0.6 + 1.2) is a very steep price to pay solely for the discipline a good advisor can provide as part of his or her overall service.[108]

Financial Advisory Firms Can Add Value

The following list identifies ways that a good financial advisory firm can add value to your portfolio and questions you should ask when interviewing prospective firms.

- Do you provide continuing access to the latest academic research on the financial markets? It was just a few years ago, for example, that the value effect was uncovered. A good advisory firm will continue to educate its clients through conferences, seminars, and/or newsletters.

- Do you integrate an investment plan into a complete estate and tax plan? Tax strategies play an important part in determining the return on your portfolio, as well as the preservation of the value of the estate you are able to pass on to your heirs. The advisory firm should be able to act as quarterback for your financial services team, which might include, among others, your accountant, attorney, and life insurance agent.

- Do you establish an investment policy that incorporates my unique tolerance for risk and investment time horizon?

- Do you develop an appropriate model portfolio and appropriate asset allocation, perform the stomach acid and liquidity tests, insure that the appropriate "devil's advocate" questions are asked, and help select the specific investment vehicles?

- Are you available on an ongoing basis to discuss whether the investment policy remains appropriate over time and as personal circumstances change?

- Do you provide access to institutional-style passive asset class funds not available to the general public?

- Will you provide the discipline, during both good and bad times, to help me stick with the strategy? An investment advisor should be able to take the emotion out of the decision-making process.

- Do you provide expertise over a broad range of financial issues, such as what type of mortgage to use when buying a home, or whether a variable annuity is appropriate?

- Do you provide creative approaches, such as the laddered portfolio method, to meeting cash flow needs and to developing solutions for financial problems?

- Will you track the performance of my portfolio and insure that the rebalancing process is performed on a regular basis and in a cost- and tax-efficient manner?

- Do you provide regular reporting, at least on a quarterly basis, that clearly communicates the performance of the portfolio?

- Do you provide the time to do all these things?

- Finally, do you build trust, get to personally know the client, and establish rapport along with a high level of comfort?

The Checklist

If you hire an investment advisory firm, here is another checklist you will find useful.

- The investment philosophy of the advisory firm should be consistent with your own. By now I would hope that philosophy means a commitment to diversified, global, passive asset class investing, based on Modern Portfolio Theory. The advisory firm should require, and specifically sign off on, a jointly developed investment policy statement.

- The investment advisory firm should be independent of any potential conflicts of interests, such as earning commissions from the sale of products it recommends. The firm should do business on a fee-only basis. This is the only way to insure that your advisor's interests are aligned with your own.

- The firm should have a team with which you are comfortable. No one individual has all the knowledge and skills necessary to be able to assist over the entire spectrum of the categories just listed. In addition, you may need advice at a time when one particular individual is not available; and, unfortunately, one particular individual may not always be there. This is another reason why an investment policy statement is important. If your main contact is unavailable, by reviewing the investment policy statement any of the firm's advisors will quickly be able to understand your situation and provide the appropriate response. The firm should be committed to a team approach, and you should interview more than just one individual.

- You should perform a careful due diligence on the firm and its principals. You should do thorough reference checks and make sure that both the firm and its individual members have the appropriate licenses.

- The firm should be able to demonstrate to you that it can add value in a way that more than justifies its fees.

There are two final recommendations. First, never give an advisor a general power of attorney without first seeking legal counsel. It is generally not necessary and can often lead to trouble. The custodian (the institution responsible for physically holding your assets and for keeping appropriate records) of your investment account should only disburse funds to accounts that only you control. You should also receive confirmations of all transactions. A limited power of attorney, allowing the advisor to execute your instructions, as well as to access your account information from the custodian, is sufficient.

Second, make sure that your assets are kept in custody by a financially strong institution with a good reputation for customer service. The custodian should be sufficiently insured to cover the value of your account.

An effective advisor can add value equal to many times his or her fee. For example, just by providing access to institutional-style passive asset class funds an advisor can add 3–4 percent per annum, or more, to your returns. The advisor can also help by simply preventing you from making some very poor investment decisions.

Sound financial advice is not expensive, especially when measured against the value an advisor can add. The typical investment advisory firm charges between 1 percent and 2 percent per annum, based on the amount of assets under management. For very large accounts, fees are generally negotiated to below 1 percent. When comparing fees be sure you are comparing apples to apples, as some firms only provide investment advice, while others provide a broader array of services, including estate and tax planning, within their fee structure. Finally, remember that while good advice may not be cheap, it is far less expensive than bad advice.

CHAPTER 11

♦

Summary

Success is a journey, not a destination. —Ben Sweetland

It is the difference of opinion that makes horse races.
—Mark Twain, *Pudd'nhead Wilson*

You'll never get much of an argument against the low-cost indexing approach from us. —*Morningstar Investor,* July 1997

We have now come to the end of the road. A brief summary and review of what Wall Street does not want you to know is appropriate.

- Markets are generally highly efficient!

- While it is not impossible to outperform an efficient market, the odds of it being done, even by professionals, are very low.

- Because past performance is not a reliable predictor of future performance, it is impossible to forecast which money managers and market gurus will be the lucky few.

- The question of whether or not markets are efficient is an interesting academic question. However, the real question facing investors is whether the correct strategy is active or passive management. I've given clear evidence that even when market inefficiencies may exist, markets are not so inefficient that active managers can overcome the costs of their efforts and the taxes generated by their trading activity.

- With institutions now controlling a market share approaching 90 percent of all trading, the competition among professionals is too tough, thereby making active management nonproductive.

- Efforts to time the market are doomed to fail, because so much of the action occurs over very brief time frames.

- The use of active managers causes an investor to lose control of the asset allocation decision, the single most important determinant of the expected return and risk of a portfolio. Active managers expose investors to style drift, which can have unanticipated and nasty consequences.

- Most of what is published by trade publications and the rating services and aired by so-called financial experts is really nothing more than investment pandering. To attach anything other than entertainment value to such reports can be dangerous to your economic health. These experts are all part of the 6 percent solution—the loser's game—hyped by Wall Street because it is in its best interest, not yours.

- Investors can easily adopt the winner's game, the investment strategy carrying the banner of a Nobel Prize and called Modern Portfolio Theory.

The only way to win the loser's game of active management: Don't play! Rather than attempt to time the market or pick individual stocks, it is more productive to invest and stay invested. As Warren Buffett said: "We continue to make more money when snoring than when active." Mr. Buffett also said, "Most investors, both institutional and individual, will find that the best way to own common stocks is through an index fund that charges minimal fees. Those following this path are sure to beat the net results (after expenses and fees) delivered by the great majority of investment professionals."[109]

Economics professors Dwight Lee and James Verbrugge of the University of Georgia explain the power of the efficient markets theory in the following manner.

The efficient markets theory is practically alone among theories in that it becomes more powerful when people discover serious inconsistencies between it and the real world. If a clear efficient market anomaly is discovered, the behavior (or lack of behavior) that gives rise to it will tend to be eliminated by competition among investors for higher returns. . . . [For example,] if stock prices are found to follow predictable seasonable patterns . . . this knowledge will elicit responses that have the effect of eliminating the very patterns that they were designed to exploit. . . . The implication is striking. The more the empirical flaws that are discovered in the efficient markets theory the more robust the theory becomes. Those who do the most to ensure that the efficient market theory remains fundamental to our understanding of financial economics are not its intellectual defenders, but those mounting the most serious empirical assault against it![110]

The starting point for implementing the winning strategy is to buy passively managed funds such as index funds. Index funds, particularly institutional, passively managed funds, assure investors that they will receive a market rate of return in a tax-efficient manner.

Markets compensate investors with returns commensurate with the degree of risk they take. By investing in asset classes that are higher risk, and therefore higher return, an investor can actually outperform the market as a whole. These higher risk, higher expected return asset classes are small-capitalization stocks, value stocks, and small value stocks. An investor can reduce portfolio risk by investing in a group of broad, global, diversified, passive asset class funds. This strategy dampens volatility and produces higher returns. Using the stomach acid and liquidity tests, as well as the asset allocation time horizon guideline, an investor can build a portfolio that will meet his or her unique investment time horizon and risk profile.

Investing in equities is risky only if your investment horizon is short. Investors should think of losses as temporary and gains as permanent. Bear markets are really just periods when the market temporarily wears a big "For Sale" sign. On July 8, 1932, the DJIA recorded an intraday low of 40. Sixty-five years later it had grown almost two hundred times. As Nick Murray says: "Success is purely a function of two things: (1) recognition of the inevitability of major market declines; and (2) emotional/behavioral preparation to regard such declines as . . . non-events."[111]

An investor should avoid an investment strategy that is too conservative by using the laddered portfolio approach. Once you build a suitable portfolio, there is a need for regular checkups of both your personal situation (ability, as opposed to willingness, to accept risk) and the performance of the portfolio. You should regularly rebalance your portfolio in order to prevent market movements from shifting your risk profile through style drift. Disciplined rebalancing maintains the investor's risk profile and actually improves investment returns by buying low and selling high. Aggressive investors can use the strategy of "regressing to the mean" to try to enhance returns (see appendix A). Having developed a portfolio, the investor should allocate assets between taxable and tax-deferred accounts.

A formal investment policy statement should be drawn up to

serve as a guide for you and your investment advisor. In searching for an investment advisor who can add value, during the interview you should use the checklist provided. Finally, investors who have portfolios with large unrealized gains need not be trapped into inaction by their desire, correct as it may be, to defer taxes (see appendix B).

Clearly, it is very difficult to beat the market. As technology and the ability to process information continue their rapid progress, I believe it will only become more difficult to do so. With so many practitioners trying, some will inevitably succeed. But investors should not rely on the past performance of those who have previously beaten the market, because past success has historically been a very poor predictor of future success.

If you do manage to find an active manager who has beaten the market, check to see if he or she has done so on an after-tax basis. Then check his or her asset allocation. If an active manager has managed to beat the market, it is highly probable he or she invested in the high-return asset classes of small-cap, value, or small value stocks. The following study backs up this assertion.

A study of some nine hundred growth and growth and income funds from 1988 to 1994 found that the returns posted by managers with degrees from universities whose entering students have high SAT scores—such as the Ivy League colleges—beat competitors from lower ranked schools by more than a full percentage point. Younger managers and MBA holders also outperformed their older and non-MBA rivals.

The reason behind the superior performance was both simple and predictable. The researchers found that "high SAT" managers and those with MBAs tended to invest in high-risk, high-return stocks! Sound familiar? You don't need an MBA and you don't have to pay an active money manager large fees to generate superior returns. All you really need is a faith that markets work—that risks and returns are highly correlated.[112]

Investors also need to beware of studies that claim that active managers do beat their benchmarks. The studies I have seen that make this claim have been "polluted" by what is called survivorship bias; that is, unsuccessful funds usually are made to disappear before their performance becomes embarrassing. In the most comprehensive study ever done on mutual funds, covering the period 1962–1993, Mark Carhart found that by 1993 fully one-third of all funds in his sample had disappeared. This shows how important survivorship bias is.[113] "In 1996 alone 242 (5 percent) of the 4,555 stock funds tracked by Lipper Analytical Services Inc. were merged or liquidated. Such disappearances caused Lipper's fund-performance averages, like wine and cheese, to improve with age. In 1986, Lipper reported that 568 stock funds delivered an average 1986 return of 13.39 percent. Today, Lipper puts the average 1986 return at 14.65 percent."[114] The reason for the improvement is that 134 (24 percent) of the original 568 funds were made to disappear. For example, if a provider of a family of funds has two small-cap funds, and one is performing poorly, the provider will merge the poorly performing one into the stronger one, simply making the poor performance disappear. Another Lipper Analytic Services study produced the following results: "The return of all general equity funds for the ten-year period studied was 15.69 percent, which was 1.5 percent below that of the funds that existed at the end of the period (the survivors) and almost 2 percent below the return of the S & P 500 Index."[115] "Over the fifteen-year period ending December 1992 the annual return of all equity mutual funds was 15.6 percent per annum. When you include all the funds that failed to survive the entire period the annual return dropped to 14.8 percent. The cumulative difference in returns was 781 percent versus 689 percent."[116]

Summary

Thanks to an unfortunate decision by the Securities and Exchange Commission (SEC), investors now have to contend with more fairy tales when analyzing mutual fund performance. Until now, investors had to only contend with the aforementioned problem of survivorship bias. The SEC has now given permission to mutual funds to report the preinception performance of "incubator funds" in their historical performance figures. This ruling gives the industry carte blanche to create dozens of funds, seed them with their own capital, and then take public only the few that rack up good performance records. The same fund manager could be given three funds to manage and then take public only the one winner. The two losers would simply disappear, as if they never existed. Another problem is that these incubator funds will have reduced operating expenses, including no advertising expenses and probably lower management fees, further distorting reality.

This unfortunate ruling provides the Wall Street establishment with ammunition to keep alive the myth that active managers can add value. Unfortunately for uninformed investors, the story is unlikely to have a fairy tale's happy ending.

In fairness to the popular press, they do occasionally acknowledge the advantages of passively managed funds. Tyler Mathisen, the executive editor of *Money* magazine, writes, "Bogle [of the Vanguard group of funds, the largest provider of retail index funds] wins: Index funds should be the core of most portfolios today."[117] And columnist Susan Lee of *Worth* magazine writes, "The index fund is a truly awesome invention. A cheap S & P 500 or a Wilshire 5000 Index fund ought to constitute at least half of your portfolio."[118] The only problem with these statements is that neither magazine will give passive management a wholehearted endorsement. If passively managed funds (i.e., index funds) are so good, why shouldn't they be the only ones an investor should use? These magazines withhold such wholehearted endorsement for two reasons. First, if the magazine's readers believed in passive management, who would buy magazines touting which stocks and mutual funds to buy? Second, these magazines carry a great amount of advertising from actively managed mutual funds. They would not want to lose valuable advertising revenue. You must remember whose interests they have at heart.

I have attempted to explain the concepts of Modern Portfolio Theory in a way that every reader can understand. John Bogle performed a great service by breaking down this complex body of work into two obvious facts:

1. Since all investors collectively own the entire stock market, if passive investors—holding all stocks, forever—can match the gross return of the stock market, [because the whole must equal the sum of the parts,] active investors, as a group, can do no better. They too must match the gross return of the stock market.

2. Since the management fees and transaction costs incurred by passive investors are substantially lower than those incurred by active investors, and both provide equal gross returns, then passive investors must earn higher net returns.[119]

In addition to Bogle's insights, remember that passive managers are more tax efficient due to their lower turnover. As a result, passive investors as a group earn higher after-tax returns than active investors.

As Bogle stated, "As the logicians would say, QED. So it is demonstrated."[120]

My fondest wish is that you have found this book not only educational but practical. Information is worth very little if you do not know how to use it. I have tried to provide you with all the information you need to improve your investment results and give you the tools with which to accomplish that objective. I also tried to make it an enjoyable experience. I now know the hard work that goes into writing a book. (How anyone did so prior to the advent of personal computers and word processing software is beyond me.) Nevertheless, I hope you had as much fun reading it as I had writing it. Debunking legends can be lots of fun.

A fitting conclusion to this book are the comments of two noted financial experts. At an economic forecasting conference, Steve Forbes quoted his grandfather, who founded the magazine eighty years ago: "You make more money selling the advice than following it."[121] Finally, Jonathan Clements of the *Wall Street Journal* offered these two pieces of advice: "Ignore market timers, Wall Street strategists, technical analysts, and bozo journalists who make market predictions. Admit to your therapist that you can't beat the market."[122]

I have introduced you to Modern Portfolio Theory and its associated investment strategies. I know of no better way to describe my hopes for your relationship with this powerful knowledge than to recall what Humphrey Bogart said to Claude Rains in the last scene from *Casablanca* as they faded into the mist. "I think this is the beginning of a beautiful friendship."

Epilogue

When I was born, my father did a brilliant thing. He took the $500 I had received as gifts and bought one share of each of 10 different stocks. By the time I was 10, right after I had finished reading about how my hero Mickey Mantle was doing in his pursuit, along with Roger Maris, of the legendary Babe Ruth's home run record, I would turn to the financial section of the *New York Times* to see how my portfolio was doing. People were amazed to see a 10-year-old reading the *Times*, let alone the financial section.

I became so fascinated with the financial markets that I eventually earned a BBA in finance from Baruch College, which is part of the City University of New York. I then went on to receive an MBA from New York University, majoring in international finance and trade theory. While there, my studies covered much of the work that is now called Modern Portfolio Theory.

After a two-year stint as manager of international finance at CBS (the parent of the television network), I moved to Citicorp, where for 10 years I advised multinational corporations on the management of financial risk. As a regional treasurer for Citicorp, I managed a multibillion-dollar deposit position, ran one of the bank's largest foreign exchange trading rooms, and served as an economic advisor to multinational companies. I then joined Prudential Home Mortgage as vice-chairman, where I was responsible for financial risk management and served as chief economist for the company.

I gave many speeches to the executives of our large corporate clients on the economic outlook for the United States. I have also lectured at Stanford University. I have even appeared on *CNBC*, which certainly qualifies me as a "market expert." Presently, I am a principal in Buckingham Asset Management (BAM), an investment advisory firm that manages other people's money, as well as the investment funds of all of its principals. My purpose in telling you all this is not to impress you or to establish my credentials as the author of this book. Instead, it sets the stage for this simple story.

My friends, business associates, and clients often ask for my opinion on the state and direction of the financial markets. They know that I always have an opinion and am willing to provide the listener with as much detail as he or she wants. While I am willing to offer my opinion, I quickly point out that I never base my own investment decisions on my opinion, and neither should they. If I acted on my own opinions, I would be playing the loser's game, just as I once did on the tennis court. I now know how to play the winner's game, in both tennis and investing. If I have accomplished what I set out to do when I first sat down to write this book, you, too, will have learned this lesson. I cannot do any better a job at forecasting the direction of markets than anyone else (at least not enough to be able to outperform a well-diversified portfolio of institutional-style passive asset class mutual funds). I have learned that the markets are efficient, and while it is not impossible to beat the market, the odds of success are so low and the cost of failure so high that it does not make sense to try. Another way to think about this situation is: Why even try, when you can just let the markets work for you? All you have to do is believe that markets work—in other words, believe in the capitalist system. With the fall of the Soviet Union, I believe there are now only three groups left in the world that do not believe that markets work—the North Koreans, the Cubans, and active managers. How's that for good company? (For good measure, you can throw in Dick Gephardt.)

A few other brief pieces of advice:

- "Don't invest in new or 'interesting' investments. They are designed to be sold to investors, not to be owned by investors."[123]

- "If you find yourself tempted to ask the question what stock should I buy, resist the temptation. If you do ask, don't listen. And if you hear an answer, promise yourself that you will ignore it."[124]

If you follow the advice provided in his book, you can tell everyone that your investment approach is the same as the one used by the most sophisticated institutional investors. And if you build a globally diversified portfolio consisting solely of passively managed asset class mutual funds, each of which probably owns hundreds, perhaps thousands, of different stocks, the next time you are at a cocktail party and someone tries to dazzle you with a story about some great stock they bought, you can say, "I own that too." The odds are that you probably do.

The Library

One of the reasons I decided to write this book is that I found no comprehensive book that explained to the average investor how markets work, why they work the way they do, and how to make them work for you. I tried to accomplish these objectives and to provide some very specific guidance on ways you can implement what you have learned. I hope I have succeeded.

In my research, I came across several books that I believe should be read by every investor. They are all written in a way that can provide value to every reader. These books are: Peter Bernstein's *Capital Ideas* and his *Against the Gods; The Portable MBA in Investing*, edited by Peter Bernstein; John Bogle's *Bogle on Mutual Funds*; Charles Ellis's *Investment Policy*; and Burton Malkiel's *A Random Walk Down Wall Street*. I would also like to recommend an excellent work, Frank Armstrong's *Investment Strategies for the Twenty-first Century*, which is available on the Internet.

I would like to note that I owe a special thanks to Charles Ellis. His book provided the link between understanding the winner and loser games of tennis and the winner and loser games in the world of investing.

I hope I have lived up to the standards set by these authors.

The Modern Portfolio Theory Challenge

Whenever my firm meets with a potential client, we always conclude our presentation with the following challenge.

"Take our presentation to your current advisor, whomever they might be. If they can show you even one good reason, backed by any credible academic study, that you should not utilize the strategies described in our presentation, for at least the core (vast majority) of your investment portfolio, we will walk away from your business."

To date, no one has beaten the Modern Portfolio Theory challenge.

Epilogue

EXHIBIT A.
Results of the Largest Corporate Pension Funds

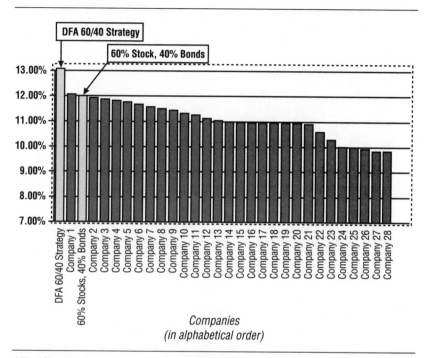

Companies
(in alphabetical order)

Allied-Signal Inc.	Dow Chemical Co.	McDonnell Douglas Corp.
American Telephone &	Du Pont de Nemours & Co.	Nynex Corp.
Telegraph	Eastman Kodak Co.	Pacific Telesis Group
Ameritech Corp.	Ford Motor Co.	Phillip Morris Companies
Bell Atlantic Corp.	General Dynamics Corp.	Inc.
BellSouth Corp.	General Electric Co.	Sears, Roebuck & Co.
Boeing Co.	General Motors Corp.	Southwestern Bell Corp.
Caterpillar Inc.	GTE Corp.	United Technologies Corp.
Chevron Corp.	IBM Corp.	U S West Corp.
Chrysler Corp.	Lockheed Corp.	USX Corp.

Sources: Piscataqua Research, Inc., Portsmouth, N.H., and Dimensional Fund Advisors Inc.

Epilogue

EXHIBIT B.
Emerging Markets Mutual Funds
Three-Year Returns Ending December 1996
Annualized Compound Returns (%)

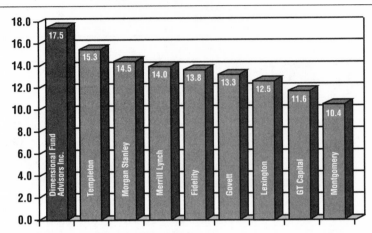

Sources: Morningstar and Dimensional Fund Advisors

EXHIBIT C.
EMERGING MARKETS STRATEGY
ANNUAL RETURN

	Argentina	Brazil	Indonesia	Malaysia	Mexico	Portugal	Thailand	Turkey
1988	34.47	157.00	248.24	18.88	89.91	−30.26	35.74	−69.60
1989	108.16	20.47	26.20	58.83	71.20	35.84	123.62	366.86
1990	−26.34	−71.44	−1.16	−10.49	36.63	−28.61	−29.43	16.15
1991	360.06	269.39	−43.47	11.86	118.91	−6.05	16.44	−26.26
1992	−24.71	−1.56	6.65	20.61	21.71	−24.70	24.52	−46.08
1993	53.44	105.54	110.49	91.97	48.67	32.74	88.40	202.70
1994	−23.76	59.90	−23.66	−19.69	−42.64	23.64	−17.96	−50.43
1995	2.56	−13.63	4.92	3.05	24.89	−9.27	−6.11	− 4.67

Simulated Data Period January	1988–1995
Average annualized return, eight countries	18.14%
Equal-weight strategy with annual rebalancing	29.72%
Equal-weight strategy with monthly rebalancing	31.57%

Source: International Finance Corporation

240

Appendix A

REGRESSING TO THE MEAN: A STRATEGY FOR THE AGGRESSIVE INVESTOR

As discussed in Chapter 9, rebalancing not only maintains your risk profile but also improves returns. The aggressive investor, willing to accept more risk, and the pain that greater volatility can generate, has an alternative strategy that can improve the returns of straight rebalancing. The strategy is based on the belief that over long periods of time asset class returns will "regress to their mean," and on the fact that even asset classes that produce similar returns over long periods of time will, nonetheless, produce returns that may vary significantly over shorter periods of time.

A simple example explains the concept of regressing to the mean. If an asset class that is expected to produce returns of 10 percent per annum produces returns below 10 percent for a period of time, then future returns are expected to exceed 10 percent in order for the long-term return to average 10 percent. In producing returns above the long-term expected rate, the rate of return for the entire period will have regressed to the mean, or returned to the average.

Small-cap and value asset classes have produced similar returns over very long time periods. The returns they have produced, however, have varied significantly from year to year, or even decade to decade. Asset classes move in and out of favor. Since we cannot predict which asset class will be the star performer, we do not put all our eggs in one basket. We diversify, and rebalance. Real estate, for example, was the star performer in the 1970s and early 1980s and a very poor performer through 1995. In 1996 it was the top-performing asset class. With the knowledge that while asset class returns will vary but eventually regress to their mean, one can develop an aggressive strategy that should produce higher returns.

Let us say that a certain portfolio consists of only two asset classes, A and B. Because they have similar risk characteristics, they have produced similar returns of 10 percent per annum over a long period of time. Using a 50/50 allocation, $1,000 is invested in each asset class. Assume that after one year the value of A has increased 20 percent to $1,200, while the value of B has remained unchanged at $1,000. The total portfolio increased by 10 percent, from $2,000 to $2,200. The asset allocation shifted from 50/50 to 55 percent A/45 percent B, and it is time to rebalance. In the previous examples I explained that in order to restore the original allocation one needs to sell $100 of A and buy $100 of B. I will now examine a more aggressive alternative.

Since one expects that over time the returns of asset classes A and B will be similar, one must therefore expect that B, in order to make up for its recent underperformance, will outperform A in the future. With this expectation, one would sell enough of A and buy enough of B to reverse their current allocations. In other words, one would sell $200 of A and buy $200 of B. One would then have a portfolio consisting of $1,000 of A and $1,200 of B, reversing the allocation that the market's movement produced in that time period. Instead of returning the portfolio to a 50/50 allocation, one will reverse the allocation from 55 percent A/45 percent B to 45 percent A/55 percent B.

Let us examine the effect of this strategy if the asset classes do regress to their mean returns of 10 percent in the ensuing time period. Asset class A would remain unchanged in value after growing 20 percent in the first year, while asset class B would grow in value by 20 percent after remaining unchanged in the prior period. If one performed normal rebalancing, the portfolio would have grown to $2,420 ($1,100 in A remaining unchanged and $1,100 in B growing 20 percent to $1,320). Alternatively, the more aggressive regressing-to-the-mean strategy would have caused the portfolio to grow to $2,440 ($1,000 in A remaining unchanged in value and $1,200 in B growing 20 percent to $1,440). The portfolio's return was enhanced by a more aggressive version of the buy low and sell high strategy.

The following table, produced by Morningstar in 1994, is a powerful illustration of the regressing-to-the-mean strategy at work.

Objective	Five Years to March 1989	Five Years to March 1994
International stocks	20.6%	9.4%
Income	14.3%	11.2%
Growth and income	14.2%	11.9%
Growth	13.3%	13.9%
Small company	10.3%	15.9%
Aggressive growth	8.9%	16.1%
Average	13.6%	13.1%

The average performance in both periods was almost identical, but the reverse order in terms of performance is almost too good to be true.[125]

Appendix A

While this strategy should produce higher returns, investors must be aware that they are varying from their carefully chosen asset allocations and have altered their risk profiles. They should expect greater volatility in addition to greater expected returns. Another factor to consider is that a regressing-to-the-mean strategy, because it involves buying and selling larger amounts of assets, will incur greater transaction costs and greater income taxes. The greater transaction costs and the greater tax costs may exceed the benefits of this more aggressive tactic. Because of these issues, a regressing-to-the-mean approach to rebalancing may only be appropriate for use in tax-deferred accounts. It should also be used only by very aggressive investors. As with any rebalancing strategy, an investor must be prepared to stick with this approach for long periods of time, since asset classes can stay out of favor for long periods of time.

One final note: A simplified version of the regressing-to-the-mean strategy can be adopted by anyone. Whenever new money is available, invest it in the asset classes that performed the worst over the most recent period. As long as your asset allocation does not get too far out of line from your original strategy, you should remain comfortable.

Appendix B

HOW TO ANALYZE THE HOLD OR SELL DECISION—TRAPPED BY A LOW TAX BASIS?

The greatest of all gifts is the power to estimate things at their true worth.
                                                        —La Rochefoucauld

You are convinced that passive asset class investing is the way to invest the core, if not all, of your portfolio. Unfortunately, you are currently invested in actively managed funds. The only thing preventing you from selling these funds and investing the proceeds in a passively managed portfolio is that your current portfolio has a low tax basis, and you do not want to pay the capital gains tax. You prefer to continue to defer the tax on the unrealized capital gain. What to do? (Of course, if your funds are in a tax-advantaged account, like an IRA, this is not an issue.)

The first thing you should do is check to see if you really have a tax problem. Many investors forget to add reinvested distributions (on which taxes have already been paid) into their cost basis. Once you have done so, the gain may not be as large as you thought. If you still have a big gain, I suggest that you investigate whether or not it is still advantageous to sell your actively managed funds, pay the requisite taxes now, and reinvest the proceeds into a passively managed asset class portfolio. Use the following example as a guide.

Assume that you have a portfolio of actively managed funds with a current value of $200,000 and a tax basis of $150,000. Assuming a total state and federal capital gains tax of 30 percent, you would pay a tax of $15,000 ($50,000 × 30 percent), leaving you with only $185,000 to reinvest. While it is known that actively managed funds have a very difficult time matching the S & P 500 Index, assume that your funds will be among the few lucky ones to do so, at least on a pretax basis.

Now analyze the hold or switch decision. Since after-tax returns are the only ones that matter, assume that, conservatively, you lose only 1 percent per annum to taxes. If your fund is one with a very high turnover, I would use a figure of 2 percent or 3 percent. While I have shown that over the past 20 years an all-equity model portfolio has outperformed the S & P 500 Index by over 4 percent per annum, assume that our new portfolio will outperform the S & P 500 Index by only 2 percent. This brings the total by which your passive asset class portfolio is expected to outperform your old actively managed portfolio to 3 percent per annum (1 percent in tax efficiency and 2 percent in higher returns).

One can now estimate how long it will take to recoup the lost tax dollars. We take the $185,000 available for investment and multiply it by the 3 percent expected improvement in returns; the annual benefit is $5,500. Dividing this figure into $15,000, we arrive at a break-even point of just under three years. If our new $185,000 portfolio grew at a 13 percent rate over the next three years, it would increase to about $267,000. The $200,000 portfolio, growing at a 10 percent rate, would increase to about $266,000. Given the other benefits provided by the passive asset class strategy, including gaining control over the asset allocation decision, and given that history tells us that the 3 percent improvement in returns may in fact be conservative, this decision should be easy. The conclusion: You may not be as trapped as you think. I would suggest that the switch should be made at any break-even point of seven years or less.

It is worth noting that had we used 4 percent as our expected improvement in pretax returns (which is closer to the historical performance differential with the S & P 500 Index), and 2 percent for the tax effect, for a total of 6 percent, the break-even point would be less than 18 months. The expected percentage performance differential to use is up to you.

Appendix C

EVEN WITH A CRYSTAL BALL . . .

Probably the most remarkable and revealing story on relying on trade publications for advice is the following tale; it also provides valuable insight into the skills of active managers and their ability to beat a passive strategy. Each year *Business Week* (*BW*) and *Forbes* (*F*) publish their "Best Buy" list of U.S. mutual funds. Their recommendations are broken down into major asset classes including U.S. small-cap, U.S. small-cap value, U.S. large-cap, and U.S. large-cap value. A portfolio can be constructed with an equal weighting of 25 percent for each of these asset classes and an equal weighting of the recommended funds within each asset class. Using the Morningstar database, a comparison can then be made between the performance of these active managers with the performance of an equivalent portfolio of passively man-aged asset class funds for the period January 1992–December 1996. Presumably, the funds that made the Best Buy lists had produced superior performance.

In other words, if you went back in time to January 1992 and

Appendix C

had a crystal ball that allowed you to see the 1997 Best Buy lists, you could create a portfolio of the Best Buy funds. (To compare the performance of the crystal ball's Best Buy portfolio with a passive asset class strategy, I have used DFA passive asset class funds for the periods that they were available, and the CRSP asset class indices for the remaining periods.)

Business Week and *Forbes* Best Buys
Versus
Passive Asset Class Strategy

Five-Year Annualized Returns
January 1992–December 1996

Funds	Returns (%)	Average Return of "Best Buy" Funds (%)
Small-cap		
Acorn Fund (*BW, F*)	17.6	
Baron Asset Fund (*BW, F*)	20.0	
Managers Special Equity (*BW*)	17.4	
DFA 9–10	**19.5**	18.33
Small-cap value		
Fidelity Low Priced Stock (*BW*)	20.8	
Franklin Balance Sheet Invest. (*BW*)	18.9	
Linder Growth Fund—Investor (*F*)	14.3	
Skyline Fund—Special Equities (*F*)	20.6	
DFA Small Value Fund*	**20.8**	18.65
Large-cap value		
Babson Value Fund (*BW, F*)	18.6	
Dodge & Cox Stock Fund (*F*)	17.6	
Fidelity Destiny I (*BW*)	19.8	
Fidelity Equity—Income Fund (*BW, F*)	17.4	
Oppenheimer Quest Opportunity A (*BW*)	18.5	
Safeco Income Fund (*F*)	14.9	
Vanguard/Windsor II (*F*)	16.7	
DFA Large Value Fund**	**20.8**	17.64

*CRSP Sm. Value Index from 1/92–3/93
**CRSP Lrg. Value Index from 1/92–3/93

Appendix C

Funds	Returns (%)	Average Return of "Best Buy" Funds (%)
Large-cap growth		
Columbia Growth Fund (*F*)	15.1	
Dreyfus Appreciation Fund (*BW, F*)	13.6	
Fidelity Growth Company (*F*)	14.1	
Harbor Capital Appreciation (*F*)	13.5	
Phoenix Growth A (*BW*)	10.5	
Vanguard US Growth Portfolio (*BW, F*)	12.9	
DFA Large Co. Fund	**14.9**	13.28

Total Return	Passive/Managed Portfolio	"Best Buy" Portfolio
	19.0	17.00

Source: *Business Week*, February 3, 1997
Forbes, February 10, 1997

Your actively managed portfolio produced an annualized return of 17 percent. Not a bad performance, except for the fact that it underperformed the passively managed portfolio by a full 2 percent per annum. Even with the benefit of a crystal ball, the Best Buy funds underperformed a passively managed strategy. In addition to producing 2 percent per annum better returns, the passive strategy was also superior from a risk-adjusted perspective. The Best Buy funds generated only about 90 percent of the returns of the passive strategy while, on average, they incurred greater volatility than the passive asset class funds. Simply put, the Best Buy portfolio produced lower returns and greater risk than did an apples-to-apples passive asset class portfolio.

If a crystal ball that enabled you to see the *Business Week* and *Forbes* issues five years before they were printed did not help you create a portfolio that outperformed a similar passively managed portfolio, are you willing to risk your investment dollars without a crystal ball?

Appendix D

HOW SAFE IS MR. ROGERS' NEIGHBORHOOD?

One of my favorite books is *Past Imperfect: History According to the Movies*, by Mark Carnes. The book examines the historical accuracy of films that have been based on historical events. Carnes argues that historical accuracy has been reshaped by the film industry. For example, he points out that "your image of Captain Bligh as someone who routinely flogged his men is incorrect." And "Thomas More was not the benevolent martyr he was portrayed to be in *A Man for All Seasons*. In fact, he shrieked for the blood of Protestants and gloated when they burned."

Just as filmmakers have reshaped our perceptions of history in order to produce marketable movies, the propaganda machines of Wall Street and the financial media have reshaped our perceptions of financial history for their own benefit. It is amazing just how much your perceptions can change when the light of historical fact has been allowed to shine through. Of course, I have already discussed the power of the U.S. press in extolling the "virtues" of active management.

With the advent of national media coverage of the financial markets by cable networks such as CNBC and CNN, a number of media stars are being created. By their mere appearance on national television, these financial commentators are given credibility as "experts." One such "expert" is Jimmy Rogers, a regular on CNBC. Mr. Rogers is also a member of the prestigious Barron's Roundtable of investors that convenes twice a year to forecast the financial markets.

Two academicians from Tulane University looked at 1,600 stock calls from the members of the Roundtable, including those of Mr. Rogers. On average, his picks gained just 2.8 percent over the 250 trading days after publication, versus 15.5 percent for a control group composed of each of the two stocks with the closest market capitalization to each of his picks. Not exactly a stellar performance versus a control group that was basically the equivalent of throwing darts! It is also worth noting that Mr. Rogers finished dead last among the seven panelists who made at least 50 recommendations.[126] How was an investor to know which of the 50 experts he should listen to, and which he should ignore?

It is not my intention to single out or ridicule Mr. Rogers. I am sure that his record is no worse than most of the "experts" and probably better than some. In fact, the recommendations from the prestigious Roundtable—which has included such famous gurus as Peter Lynch, Mario Gabelli, and John Neff—when taken as a group, provided zero value added above their benchmarks over all the periods studied (25, 50, 500, and 750 trading days).[127]

Mr. Rogers is quite entertaining when appearing on TV, but there is a difference between entertainment value and value of investment advice. Self-anointed experts should not be relied on for investment advice. Moreover, terms like "market guru" or "market expert" are akin to "plastic silverware," "airline food," and "efficient bureaucracy." They are oxymorons, or contradictions in terms. Relying on so-called experts to win the investment game gives you about as much chance of success as that of the captain of the javelin team, who, on winning the coin toss deciding who will throw first, elects to receive.

Appendix E

THE PAST REVISITED

The following is one of my favorite tales of investment pandering, because it shows how hard it is to change conventional wisdom even in the face of an overwhelming body of evidence. In a September 1958 article in *Life* magazine entitled "The People's Stock Market," Ernest Havemann contrasted the booming stock market of the time with the bearish outlook of many market gurus. The DJIA stood at 513, just below its all-time high. In a situation eerily similar to today's, stock prices were then making a mockery of the advice from so-called experts and their time-tested formulas for beating the market. Baffled by a market that kept rising in the face of unemployment and corporate dividend cuts, market experts were at a loss to explain the market's persistent strength. The following are a sample of quotes from the bewildered pros: "The market is like an Indian rope trick, it goes up but nobody can understand why." "What kind of recession is this?" Market experts were watching on the sidelines, convinced that investors would pay the price for their irrational behavior (ignoring all the conventional wisdom about how stocks were supposed to perform). "The only people who've made money this year, are the people who can't read." Then, as today, the bears had a long wait. Over three years later, at year-end 1961, the DJIA stood at 735, a gain of another 43 percent from its September 1958 level of 513.

Appendix F

THE IPO MYTH

One of the recurring themes of this book is that it is in Wall Street's interests to keep alive the myth that active management adds value. Another important myth that needs exposing is that initial public offerings (IPO) make great investments. Wall Street firms generate great fee income from these transactions. Investors seem to love them as they desperately search for the next Microsoft. Let's look at the reality of actual performance. A study covering the period 1970–1990 examined the returns from a strategy of buying every IPO at the end of the first day's closing price and then holding each investment for five years. The return provided by this strategy would have been not only just 5 percent but also 7 percent per annum less than a benchmark of an investment in companies with the same market capitalization as each IPO had on its first day of trading.

In the face of this poor performance, why do investors continue to chase the latest IPO? I believe there are two explanations:

Appendix F

1. Unless an investor happens to read scholarly publications such as the *Journal of Finance*, he or she is unlikely to be aware of the facts. It is simply not in Wall Street's interest for investors to be informed.

2. Even when informed, investors often act in what appear to be irrational ways; this case, I believe, is another example of "the triumph of hope over experience." Investors seem to be willing to accept the high probability of low returns in exchange for the small chance of a home run, or possibly even more important, a great story to tell at the next cocktail party.

Much of the poor performance of IPOs can be explained by the book-to-market factor discussed in chapter 5. IPOs tend to be low book-to-market (growth) stocks; as was noted, the risk premium for value stocks (high book-to-market) over growth stocks is in excess of 5 percent.[128]

Appendix G

THE DOGS OF THE DOW

The history of Wall Street is littered with tales of the latest and greatest investment strategy. Among the litter are the nifty-fifty, dividend yield strategy, all forms of technical analysis, the Dow Theory, and the latest fad, momentum investing. Ultimately, investors who believed in these strategies and, by definition, that the markets are inefficient, underperform the market; they then chase the next fad.

The only "fad" strategy that has any validity is the Dogs of the Dow. This strategy buys either the five or the ten most depressed stocks (either lowest price or highest yielding) of the Dow. The reason this strategy has provided superior performance is simple. The depressed Dow Dog stocks are the same distressed companies that I have called value stocks—the same risky, high book-to-market companies that have a high cost of capital. Since the markets are efficient at pricing for risk, the stocks of these companies should, and do, provide higher returns. And since these are the most distressed companies, they should provide very high returns as compensation for their very risky nature.

There are, however, three problems with this strategy. First, an investor is compounding the risk of the Dogs of the Dow by creating an undiversified portfolio. In contrast, a large value asset class strategy would own hundreds of companies. Second, a Dogs of the Dow strategy is likely to be very tax inefficient. The most popular means of executing the strategy is to buy a trust, which owns the stocks and liquidates at the end of each year. This strategy, unless deployed inside a tax-deferred account, does not allow the investor the benefits of tax deferral, which can be far more important than superior investment results. Third, Wall Street firms often charge high fees for creating the Dogs of the Dow trusts.

Conclusion: For investors willing to take on the incremental risk of a nondiversified portfolio, the Dogs of the Dow may warrant a small allocation in their portfolio, but only if it can be placed within a tax-deferred account.

Appendix H

TACTICAL ASSET ALLOCATION—
ANOTHER POPULAR DELUSION

Wall Street has created many investment strategies that hold out the hope of outperforming the market. Unfortunately for investors, the only ones benefiting from these strategies are the investment firms that charge large fees for the *potential* of superior returns. Like the emperor without any clothes, these strategies are eventually exposed to the light of reality.

One strategy that gained great popularity in the 1980s and 1990s is called Tactical Asset Allocation (TAA). This strategy was an important component of the overall plans for many pension funds. By year-end 1994, almost $50 billion of institutional funds was committed to TAA, with 11 managers having about 95 percent of the total.

The objective of TAA is to provide better than benchmark returns with (possibly) lower volatility. This would be accomplished by forecasting returns of two or more asset classes and varying the exposure (percent allocation) accordingly. Each manager would then be measured against his or her benchmark. While the benchmark might be 60 percent S & P 500 Index and 40 percent Lehman Bond Index, the manager might be allowed to have his or her allocations range from 50 percent to 65 percent for equities, 20 percent to 50 percent for bonds, and 0 percent to 45 percent for cash.

In reality, TAA is just a fancy name for market timing—which, as we have seen, is a flawed strategy. By giving it a fancy name, however, Wall Street seems able to charge high fees. The performance of the 11 managers who controlled 95 percent of the assets committed to TAA was measured for the period from January 1988 (postcrash) to September 1994. Only 5 of the 11 outperformed the benchmark, with an average underperformance of six basis points (0.06 percent) per annum. In addition, there was no diminution in volatility, with 8 of the 11 showing greater volatility than the benchmark.[129] Lower returns with greater volatility. One more myth debunked.

Appendix I

10 REASONS NOT TO
INVEST IN FIDELITY

The Wall Street establishment provides a never-ending stream of anecdotes on the folly of active investing. I have attempted to limit myself to only those tales that seemed so incredible that if you didn't read it yourself you wouldn't believe it. This one certainly fits that description.

In 1996, due to poor investment performance, Fidelity's vaunted marketing machine had come to a grinding halt. In fact, in the face of the greatest bull market in history, Fidelity experienced a long streak of net redemptions by investors. A new head of retail operations, a Mr. Hondros, was assigned. Wanting to quickly turn the tide of investment dollars, in November Mr. Hondros personally wrote the copy for a new ad with the headline: "Ten Reasons To Invest In Fidelity." Accompanying the ad was a chart comparing the performance of 10 large Fidelity funds and the S & P 500 Index over the previous one- and three-year periods. Unfortunately for Mr. Hondros, over the previous 12 months, eight of the ten Fidelity funds had trailed the index. The comparison for the three-year period was even worse, with nine of the ten Fidelity funds trailing the index.

Fidelity's own marketing managers derided the ad as "Ten Reasons Not to Invest in Fidelity." The ads were eventually pulled and replaced with ads showing Morningstar's ratings for the same funds, which placed the funds in a more favorable light. Unfortunately, as I have shown, those star ratings have virtually no value.[130]

Appendix J
1997'S TAX RATE CHANGES

One of the major themes of this book is that taxes play a very important role in the returns investors ultimately receive; making tax efficiency a major focus of a winning investment strategy. From an investment strategy perspective, the major impact of 1997's tax changes was to dramatically lower the rate on long-term capital gains from a maximum of 28 percent to 20 percent (for lower-bracket investors the rate can be as low as 10 percent). In addition, the holding period required for long-term capital gains treatment was increased from 12 months to 18 months. Further, for assets purchased after the year 2001 and held for five years, the maximum rate drops to 18 percent (for lower-bracket investors the rate can be as low as 8 percent). The effect of these changes was to widen the gap between short-term and long-term capital gains rates.

These changes have two important implications for investors. First, they place another nail in the coffin of active management. By further emphasizing the relative tax efficiency of a passive versus active strategy, the already difficult barrier active managers must overcome has been raised. Second, they give further credence to placing your tax-efficient, passively managed mutual funds into taxable accounts. These funds have low turnover rates, and therefore already are tax efficient in the sense of deferring most of their capital gains. In addition, most of their distributions are likely to be in the form of long-term capital gains which will be taxed at lower rates. On the other hand, if these funds were in an IRA, when withdrawals began they would be taxed at the much higher ordinary income rates.

Appendix K

NEWS FLASH: TOP PERFORMANCE IS A POOR INDICATOR OF FUTURE PERFORMANCE

This was the headline of a recent report released by Smith Barney's Consulting Group. I believe that issuing this report comes under the definition of chutzpah—the Yiddish expression for nerve. Since no one word can ever define a Yiddish expression, an example is needed. My favorite is that the true definition of chutzpah is when a child who has killed his parents throws himself on the mercy of the court as an orphan.

Smith Barney is one of the largest providers of retail mutual funds. On the one hand, they spend large amounts of dollars advertising the past performance records of their top-performing funds, and tout their Morningstar ratings of four and five stars. Presumably, investors will be tempted into buying these funds based upon their prior performance and the expectation that their superior performance will continue into the future. On the other hand, they publish a study the very first words of which are "One of the most common investor mistakes is choosing an investment

management firm or mutual fund based on recent top performance." As evidence that investors choose the top past performers they cited a survey of more than 3,300 mutual fund investors,
which was performed at Columbia University's Graduate School
of Business. On a scale of 1 (lowest) to 5 (highest), survey re-
spondents gave past performance a score of 4.62, far outdistanc-
ing other criteria, such as fees (2.28) and investment style (1.68).
They also cited a study by the Financial Research Corp which
found that 75 percent of net new cash flowing into mutual funds
was invested in Morningstar's four- and five-star funds.

To test the hypothesis that by purchasing shares of the recent
top-performing funds individual investors were following a winning strategy, Smith Barney studied 72 equity managers with at
least ten-year track records. The managers studied covered the
full spectrum of investment styles from large-cap to small-cap,
from value to growth, and from domestic to international. The
study's conclusion: "For all the periods studied, top performing
managers were more likely to drop to the bottom of performance
comparisons in subsequent periods than to repeat their peer-
beating performances." In fact, "the investment returns of top
quintile managers tended to plunge precipitously, while the returns of bottom quintile managers tended to rise dramatically."[131]

Sounds like chutzpah to me.

Appendix L

A MUTUAL FUND TO DROOL OVER

The little known Kothari & Warner mutual funds beat a broad market benchmark over the past three decades by about four percentage points a year. Even after adjusting for risk these funds turned in a spectacular performance. Don't bother to call your broker, or asking the fund manager for hot tips. The stocks were picked randomly by a computer.

Two professors questioned whether, based on past performance, it is possible to winnow out the good fund managers from the bad. Their conclusion: "It is darn difficult." Professor Kothari of MIT stated: "Randomness might give the appearance of someone being talented."

Kothari and Professor Jerald Warner, of the Simon School of Business at the University of Rochester, randomly put together 336 mutual funds—one a month constructed retroactively from 1964 to 1991—to do their study. Each fund changed its portfolio of stocks once a year, picked new stocks randomly, and expired after three years.

Appendix L

Professor Warner says, "Drawing inferences from performance data about stock-picking ability of fund managers is treacherous."

Investors should remember that the fact that Peter Lynch and Warren Buffett beat the market isn't evidence that markets are inefficient. As the Kothari & Warner study demonstrates, if you have enough people trying to beat the market, some will inevitably succeed. The real question is: How come with so many managers trying to beat the market there are far fewer who succeed than would be randomly expected? We will never know whether Lynch and Buffett are true investment gurus or whether they were simply the beneficiaries of random luck, like the Kothari & Warner funds. Keep this study in mind next time you marvel at the successful track record of a mutual fund manager.[132]

Appendix M

SOURCES AND DESCRIPTIONS OF DATA
FOR MODEL AND CONTROL PORTFOLIOS

One of the benefits of passive asset class management is the ability to simulate portfolio performance (because with no attempt at security selection or at market timing we know what assets were contained within a specific asset class). Wherever possible live data is used. When live data was not available simulated data was used; the allocations were courtesy of Dimensional Fund Advisors. Where no data series was available, as in the case of the emerging markets asset class prior to 1988, other data series with as close a match as possible were substituted. Once again I would like to thank DFA. The sections of this book that use control and model portfolios to demonstrate the power of Model Portfolio Theory and the importance of an individual's tolerance for risk in making asset allocation decisions would not have been possible without the permissions of the following people and organizations. I would like to thank them for their cooperation.

Appendix M

1. S & P 500—© Computed using data from *Stocks, Bonds, Bills, & Inflation 1997 Yearbook,*™ Ibbotson Associates, Chicago (annually updates work by Roger G. Ibbotson and Rex Sinquefield). Used with permission. All rights reserved.

2. Lehman Gov't/Corp Index—Lehman Brothers.

3. EAFE Index—Morgan Stanley Capital International (MSCI).

4. U.S. 6-10—*1973–June 1986* © CRSP, University of Chicago. Used with permission. All rights reserved. *June 1986–present* DFA 6-10 Portfolio.

5. U.S. small value—*1973–February 1992* Fama-French and CRSP University of Chicago. Used with permission. All rights reserved. *March 1992–present* DFA U.S. small-value portfolio.

6. U.S. large value—*1973–March 1993* Fama-French and © CRSP, University of Chicago. Used with permission. All rights reserved. *April 1993–present* DFA large value portfolio.

7. Real estate—*1973–1974* 50 percent: © CRSP, University of Chicago.Used with permission. All rights reserved; and 50 percent: Fama-French small value simulated. *1975–November 1994* Professor Donald Keim of the Wharton School, "Risk and Return in Real Estate: Evidence from a Real Estate Stock Index," *Financial Analysts Journal,* September–October 1993. *December 1994*–present DFA real estate portfolio.

8. International value—*1973–1974* 50 percent: EAFE Index; and 50 percent: international small. *1975–March 1993* Fama-French. *March 1993–June 1993* EAFE Index (substituted due to lack of data). *July 1993–present* DFA International high book-to-market and value portfolios.

9. International small—Various sources were used, including: Nomura Securities Investment Trust Management Company, Ltd., Tokyo, for the Japanese small company stocks (smaller

half of first section, Tokyo Stock Exchange); Professor Elwy Dimson and Professor Paul Marsh of the London Business School for the U.K. small company stocks (Hoare Govett Smaller Companies Index); DFA's Japan, Continental, U.K., and Pacific Rim small company portfolios; and DFA's international small company portfolio.

- *1973–March 1986* 50 percent: smaller half of Tokyo Stock Exchange; and 50 percent: Hoare Govett Smaller Companies Index.
- *April 1986* 50 percent: DFA U.K. small company portfolio; and 50 percent: smaller half of Tokyo Stock Exchange.
- *May 1986–June 1988* 50 percent: DFA U.K. small company; and 50 percent: DFA Japan small company portfolios.
- *July 1988–September 1989* 50 percent: DFA Japan; 30 percent: DFA Continental; and 20 percent: DFA U.K. small company portfolios.
- *October 1989–March 1990* 40 percent: DFA Japan; 30 percent: DFA Continental; 20 percent: DFA U.K.; and 10 percent: Pacific Rim small company portfolios.
- *April 1990–1992* 40 percent: DFA Japan; 35 percent: DFA Continental; 15 percent: DFA U.K.; and 10 percent: DFA Pacific Rim small company portfolios.
- *1993–September 1996* 35 percent: DFA Japan; 35 percent: DFA Continental; 15 percent: DFA U.K.; and 15 percent: DFA Pacific Rim small company portfolios.
- *October 1996–present* DFA international small company portfolio.

10. International small value—*1973–1974* international small as above. *1995–present* DFA international small value company portfolio.

11. Emerging markets—*1973–1987* 50 percent: international large value; and 50 percent: international small as above. *1988–February 1993* MSCI emerging markets index (equally weighed). *April 1993* DFA emerging market portfolio.

12. One-year fixed income—DFA: *1973–July 1983* simulated using CDs; *August 1983–present* DFA one-year portfolio.

13. Five-year fixed income—DFA: *1973–May 1987* simulated using U.S. treasuries with maximum maturity of five years; *June 1987–present* DFA five year fixed income portfolio.

14. Global fixed income—*1973–1986* simulated using equally weighted DFA one-, two-, and five-year strategies. *1987–November 1990* Lehman Bros. international country indices. *December 1990–present* DFA global fixed income portfolio.

Glossary

Active management   The attempt to uncover securities the rest of the market has either under- or overvalued. It is also the attempt to try to time investment decisions in order to be more heavily invested when the market is rising and less so when the market is falling.

AMEX   The American Stock Exchange.

Annualized standard deviation   See **standard deviation.**

Asset allocation   The process of determining what percentage of assets are dedicated to which specific asset classes.

Asset allocation time horizon guideline   Numerical formula used to determine the asset allocation between equities and fixed income assets based on the length of the investment time horizon.

Asset class   A group of assets with similar risk and reward characteristics. Cash, debt instruments, real estate, and equities are examples of asset classes. Within a general asset class, such as equities, there are more specific classes such as large and small companies, and domestic and international companies.

Basis point One hundred basis points equal 1 percent.

Blended portfolio A portfolio consisting of both equities and fixed income instruments, the typical allocation of which is 60 percent equities and 40 percent fixed income.

Book value An accounting term for the equity of a company. Equity is equal to assets less liabilities. It is often expressed in per share terms. Book value per share is equal to equity divided by the number of shares.

Book-value-to-market-value The ratio of the book value per share to the market price per share, or book value divided by market capitalization.

Chartist See **technical analysis**.

Data mining A technique for building predictive models of the real world by discerning patterns in masses of computer data.

EAFE Index The Europe, Australia, and the Far East Index, similar to the S & P 500 Index in that it consists of the stocks of the large companies from the EAFE countries. The stocks within the index are weighted by market capitalization.

Efficient market A state in which trading systems fail to produce returns in excess of the market's overall rate of return because everything currently knowable about a company is already incorporated into the stock price. The next piece of available information will be random as to whether it will be better or worse than the market expects. An efficient market is also one in which the costs of trading are low.

Emerging markets The capital markets of less-developed countries that are beginning to develop characteristics of developed countries, such as higher per capita income. Countries typically included in this category would be Brazil, Mexico, Thailand, Korea, and so on.

Expense ratio   The operating expenses of a fund expressed as a percentage of total assets. These expenses must be subtracted from the investment performance of a fund in order to determine the return received by shareholders.

Event risk   The possibility of an unanticipated occurrence taking place.

5 percent/25 percent rule   Numerical formula used to determine the need to rebalance a portfolio.

Fundamental security analysis   The attempt to uncover mispriced securities by focusing on predicting future earnings.

Growth stock   A stock trading at a relatively (to the market overall) high price to earnings ratio because the market is anticipating relatively (to the market overall) rapid growth in earnings.

Index fund   A passively managed fund that seeks to replicate the performance of a particular index (such as the Wilshire 5000, the S & P 500, or the Russell 2000) by buying all the securities in that index, in direct proportion to their weight, by market capitalization, in that index, and holding them.

Institutional fund   A mutual fund that is not available to individual investors. Typical clients are pension and profit sharing plans and endowment funds.

Institutional-style fund   A mutual fund that is available to individual investors, although in a limited way, such as through registered investment advisors. These advisors require their clients to commit to the same type of disciplined, long-term, buy and hold strategy that is typical of institutional investors.

Investment pandering   Advice on market or securities values that is designed to titillate, stimulate, and excite you into action but has no basis in reality.

Investment pornography   Extreme examples of investment pandering.

Laddered portfolio A portfolio that consists of a series of fixed income instruments, one of which matures each year, or at any desired time horizon, over the desired investment period.

Leverage The use of debt to increase the amount of assets that can be acquired, for example, to buy stock. Leverage increases the riskiness of a portfolio.

Liquidity test A test that insures that sufficient liquid assets— assets that are not at risk—exist to meet near-time cash needs, as well as other potential unanticipated requirements.

Market capitalization The market price per share times the number of shares.

Modern Portfolio Theory A Nobel Prize–winning body of academic work that consists of several concepts: First, markets are too efficient to allow returns in excess of the market's over-all rate of return to be achieved through trading systems. Active management is therefore counterproductive. Second, asset classes can be expected to achieve, over sustained periods, returns that are commensurate with their level of risk. Riskier asset classes, such as small companies and value companies, will produce higher returns as compensation for their higher risk. Third, diversification across asset classes can increase returns and reduce risk. For any given level of risk, there is a portfolio that can be constructed that will produce the highest expected return. Finally, there is no right portfolio for every investor. Each investor must choose an asset allocation that results in a portfolio with an acceptable level of risk.

NASDAQ (or NASDQ) The National Association of Securities Automated Quotations. An exchange on which securities are traded. It is frequently called the over-the-counter market.

NYSE The New York Stock Exchange.

Passive asset class funds Funds that buy and hold all securities within a particular asset class. The weighting of each security within the fund is equal to its weighting, by market capitalization, within the asset class.

Passive management   A buy and hold investment strategy, specifically contrary to active management. Typically, a passively managed portfolio purchases all securities that fit a desired asset class definition. The amount purchased of each security is in proportion to its capitalization relative to the total capitalization of all securities within that asset class. Each stock is then held until it no longer fits the definition of that asset class. (For example, a small company can grow into a large company.)

Prudent Investor Rule   A doctrine imbedded within the American legal code stating that a person responsible for the management of someone else's assets must manage those assets in a manner that must be appropriate to the financial circumstance and tolerance for risk of the investor.

Rebalancing   The process of restoring a portfolio to its original asset allocations. Rebalancing can be accomplished either through adding newly investable funds or by selling portions of the best performing asset classes and using the proceeds to purchase additional amounts of the underperforming asset classes.

Registered Investment Advisor   A designation indicating that a financial consultant is registered with the appropriate state regulators and has passed the required exams.

Regressing to the mean   A more aggressive form of rebalancing, based on the assumption that over time, investment returns for distinct asset classes return to their mean, or average, return. This strategy calls for overweighting asset classes that have been relative underperformers and underweighting asset classes that have been relative outperformers.

REIT   A Real Estate Investment Trust, available to investors through the purchase of shares in them.

Glossary

Retail funds   Mutual funds that are available to the general public.

Short   The borrowing of a security for the purpose of immediately selling it. This is done with the expectation that the investor will be able to buy the security back at a later date, at a lower price.

Small companies, or small-cap stocks   Companies that fall within the bottom 20 percent of all companies when ranked by market capitalization.

Standard deviation   A measure of volatility, or risk. For example, given a portfolio with a 12 percent annualized return and an 11 percent standard deviation, an investor can expect that in 13 out of 20 annual periods (about two-thirds of the time) the return on that portfolio will fall within one standard deviation, or between 1 percent (12 percent − 11 percent) and 23 percent (12 percent + 11 percent). The remaining one-third of the time an investor should expect that the annual return will fall outside the 1–23 percent range. Two standard deviations (11 percent × 2) would account for 95 percent (19 out of 20) periods. The range of expected returns would be between −10 percent (12 percent − 22 percent) and 34 percent (12 percent + 22 percent). The greater the standard deviation, the greater the volatility of a portfolio. Standard deviation can be measured for varying time periods. For example, you can have a monthly standard deviation or an annualized standard deviation measuring the volatility for that given time frame.

Stomach acid test   A test designed to help an investor determine the appropriate allocation between equities and fixed income assets in his or her portfolio. The test asks the question, "Do you have the fortitude and discipline to stick with your predetermined investment strategy (asset allocation) when the going gets rough?" An investor should examine the worst-case historical experience for an asset allocation to see if he or she could stick with that policy if that scenario were repeated.

Strip A series of fixed income instruments with increasing maturities.

Style Drift The drifting away from the original asset allocation of a portfolio, either by the purchasing of securities outside the particular asset class a fund is trying to represent or by significant differences in performance of the various asset classes within the portfolio.

Technical analysis The art of identifying patterns from a chart of the price movement of a particular security or market. Technical analysts believe that profits above the market's overall rate of return can be earned by predicting future price movements based on past patterns. In contrast, academics believe that markets move randomly.

Turnover The trading activity of a fund as it sells securities from a portfolio and replaces them with new ones. For example, assume that a fund began the year with a portfolio of $100 million in various securities. If the fund sold $50 million of the original securities and replaced them with $50 million of new securities, it would have a turnover rate of 50 percent.

Value stocks Companies that are ranked in the top 30 percent of companies when ranked by book-to-market value.

Zero coupon bond A bond that pays no current interest. It is purchased at a discount to face value and accrues interest each year. At maturity its value will be equal to the face value.

Notes

1. *Wall Street Journal,* January 28, 1997.
2. *New York Times,* January 28, 1997.
3. *Financial Analysts Journal,* July–August 1986.
4. ABC News' *20/20,* November 27, 1992.
5. *New York Times,* March 30, 1997.
6. *New York Times,* March 30, 1997.
7. *New York Times,* March 30, 1997.
8. Quoted in Peter Bernstein, *Against the Gods.*
9. *San Francisco Chronicle,* November 24, 1996.
10. *Wall Street Journal,* May 16, 1997.
11. *Fortune,* June 23, 1997.
12. *Wall Street Journal,* September 24, 1996.
13. *New York Times* News Service, 1997.
14. *Newsweek,* August 7, 1995.
15. *Barron's* On-Line, June 2, 1997.
16. *Business Week,* May 27, 1997.
17. *Forbes,* November 4, 1996.
18. *Journal of Finance,* June 1995.
19. *American Association of Individual Investors Journal,* September 1996.
20. *Investment Advisor,* September 1994.

Notes

21. *Kiplinger's Personal Finance,* February 1997.
22. *Wall Street Journal,* April 5, 1996.
23. *Business Week,* June 16, 1997.
24. *Wall Street Journal,* July 3, 1997.
25. John Merrill, *Beyond Stocks.*
26. John Merrill, *Beyond Stocks.*
27. Philip Halpern, *Financial Analysts Journal,* July/August 1996.
28. *Wall Street Journal,* April 29, 1997.
29. *St. Louis Post Dispatch,* July 6, 1997.
30. Peter Bernstein, *Against the Gods.*
31. *Fortune,* February 17, 1997.
32. *Fortune,* July 7, 1997.
33. *Fortune,* February 17, 1997.
34. *The Portable MBA in Investing,* edited by Peter Bernstein.
35. Burton Malkiel, *A Random Walk Down Wall Street.*
36. *Smart Money,* June 1997.
37. *Smart Money,* June 1997.
38. *Ranking Mutual Funds on an After-Tax Basis,* Stanford University Center for Economic Policy Research Discussion Paper, number 344.
39. *Wall Street Journal,* June 10, 1997.
40. "Is Your Alpha Big Enough to Cover Your Taxes?" *Journal of Portfolio Management,* Spring 1993.
41. *The Portable MBA in Investing,* edited by Peter Bernstein.
42. *Advisor's Network,* April 1997.
43. *Fortune,* July 21, 1997.
44. *Institutional Investor,* May 1997.
45. *Wall Street Journal,* July 14, 1997.
46. Peter Bernstein, *Against the Gods.*
47. *Journal of Applied Economics,* Spring 1996.
48. *Financial Management,* Spring 1996.
49. *Fortune,* March 17, 1997.
50. *Journal of Portfolio Management,* Fall 1974.
51. *The Portable MBA in Investing,* edited by Peter Bernstein.
52. Charles Ellis, *Investment Policy.*
53. *Journal of Portfolio Management,* Fall 1995.
54. John Merrill, *Beyond Stocks.*
55. *St. Louis Post Dispatch,* July 11, 1997.
56. Peter Bernstein, *Against the Gods.*
57. *Wall Street Journal,* October 17, 1996.
58. John Merrill, *Beyond Stocks.*
59. *Wall Street Journal,* January 2, 1997.

Notes

60. *Wall Street Journal,* January 30, 1997.
61. *Fortune,* December 23, 1996.
62. *Wall Street Journal,* March 17, 1997.
63. *Worth,* September 1995.
64. *Fortune,* May 12, 1997.
65. Nick Murray, *The Excellent Investment Advisor.*
66. *Journal of Portfolio Management,* Fall 1995.
67. Mark M. Carhart, "On Persistence in Mutual Fund Performance," doctoral diss., University of Chicago, December 1994.
68. *Journal of Finance,* March 1997.
69. *Morningstar Investor,* June 1997.
70. Brinson, Hood and Beebower, "Determinants of Portfolio Performance," *Financial Analysts Journal,* July–August 1986.
71. Elton, Gruber, Hlavaka, and Das, "A Reinterpretation of Evidence from Managed Portfolios," *Review of Financial Studies,* vol. 6, no. 1 (1993).
72. *New York Times,* June 16, 1996.
73. *Financial Analysts Journal,* January/February 1997.
74. *Business Week,* April 4, 1997.
75. David Booth, "The Value Added of Active Management: International Single Country Funds," January 1997.
76. Blake, Elton, Gruber, *Journal of Business* 66: 1993.
77. *Journal of Investing,* Summer 1997.
78. John Bogle, *Bogle on Mutual Funds.*
79. *Journal of Investing,* Summer 1997.
80. *St. Louis Post Dispatch,* August 12, 1997.
81. *Wall Street Journal,* December 30, 1996.
82. *Journal of Finance,* March 1959.
83. Burton Malkiel, *A Random Walk Down Wall Street.*
84. *Journal of Applied Corporate Finance,* Summer 1993.
85. Return figures based on Eugene F. Fama and Kenneth R. French, "Cross-section of Expected Stock Returns," *Journal of Finance,* June 1992.
86. *Forbes,* June 17, 1996.
87. *Financial Analysts Journal,* May–June 1987.
88. *Barron's,* April 14, 1997.
89. *Financial Analysts Journal,* January–February 1993.
90. *Wall Street Journal,* February 10, 1997.
91. Blake, Elton, Gruber, *Journal of Business* 66: 1993.
92. *Financial Analysts Journal,* January–February 1993.
93. *Fortune,* April 3, 1995.
94. *Journal of Investing,* Fall 1995.
95. *Wall Street Journal,* June 17, 1997.

Notes

96. *Wall Street Journal,* January 10, 1997.

97. *Wall Street Journal,* January 10, 1997.

98. *Morningstar Investor,* August 1996.

99. *Business Week,* September 9, 1996.

100. John Merrill, *Beyond Stocks.*

101. *The Portable MBA in Investing,* edited by Peter Bernstein.

102. John Merrill, *Beyond Stocks.*

103. Peter Bernstein, *Against the Gods.*

104. *Financial Planning,* February 1997.

105. *Wall Street Journal,* October 8, 1996.

106. *Business Week,* September 16, 1996.

107. *Fee Advisor,* September/October 1996.

108. John Merrill, *Beyond Stocks.*

109. 1997 annual letter to shareholders of Berkshire Hathaway.

110. *Journal of Applied Economics,* Spring 1996.

111. Nick Murray, *The Excellent Investment Advisor.*

112. *Business Week,* March 10, 1997.

113. *Journal of Finance,* March 1997.

114. *Wall Street Journal,* April 4, 1997.

115. Burton Malkiel, *A Random Walk Down Wall Street.*

116. John Bogle, *Bogle on Mutual Funds.*

117. *Money,* August 1995.

118. *Worth,* February 1996.

119. John Bogle, *Bogle on Mutual Funds.*

120. John Bogle, *Bogle on Mutual Funds.*

121. *St. Louis Post-Dispatch,* October 4, 1997.

122. *Wall Street Journal,* December 31, 1996.

123. Charles Ellis, *Investment Policy.*

124. Andrew Tobias, *The Only Investment Book You Will Ever Need.*

125. Peter Bernstein, *Against the Gods.*

126. *Wall Street Journal,* August 12, 1996.

127. *Journal of Finance,* June 1995.

128. *Journal of Finance,* March 1995.

129. *Journal of Portfolio Management,* Fall 1996.

130. *Wall Street Journal,* August 6, 1997.

131. *Why Top Performance Is a Poor Indicator of Future Performance,* Smith Barney Consulting Group, 1997.

132. *Wall Street Journal,* November 13, 1997.

Acknowledgments

No book is ever the work of one individual. This book is no exception. First I would like to thank my partners at Buckingham Asset Management (BAM) and BAM USA, Paul Forman, Steve Funk, Ed Goldberg, Mont Levy, Len O'Bryon, Bert Schweizer, and Stuart Zimmerman for their support, encouragement, and guidance. I would particularly like to thank Bert for his help in editing the book. I would also like to note the many editorial and concept contributions of Len and Mont. Mont also contributed some original research. I would especially like to thank Nicki Brink, Tina Ebert, and Jennifer Repp for their patience in helping to put together and insert the charts, as well as assisting with the seemingly endless rewrites.

A special note of thanks goes to my good friend Larry Goldfarb, who not only provided editorial assistance but also contributed greatly to the organization and structure of the book.

The greatest contribution was made by my agent, Sam Fleischman, who, through his suggestions on structuring and his editing work added tremendously to the quality of the book. Any shortcomings are mine. I cannot imagine a better relationship between author and agent.

Many other people made valuable contributions. Among them were Ray Bard, Gigi Mahon, Michael Landau, Marvin Mosko-

Acknowledgements

witz, Truman Talley, Marlene Tuch, Shannon Rye Wall, Roy Williams, Philip Yee, Barry Yellin, and David Zenoff. I would be remiss if I did not give a special note of thanks to Dana Stephens for all the technical computer support he provided. Without him there would never have been a manuscript.

I would also like to thank the people at Dimensional Fund Advisors. They provided the source for much of the material and anecdotes in the book. A special thanks to Weston Wellington of DFA. I have learned much from him. He seems to always be able to explain difficult concepts in an easy and often humorous way. Weston was the source of much of the humor in the book. I would also like to thank Bo Cornell of DFA for his assistance.

A special thanks goes to the over five thousand employees of Prudential Home Mortgage and Residential Services Corporation of America. Their dedication, team spirit, and commitment to excellence created a company that, in my opinion, was in many ways in a class by itself in the mortgage industry. The result of their efforts was that I had the time to write this book. It was a pleasure and privilege to work with such a fine group of people.

Finally, I would like to thank my family. First, my three children, Jodi, Jennifer, and Jacquelyn, for allowing me to monopolize our computer for about one year. I would especially like to thank the love of my life, my wife, Mona. She showed tremendous patience in reading and rereading the numerous drafts. If the book manages to make clear difficult concepts, she deserves the credit. I would also like to thank her for her tremendous support and understanding for the lost weekends, and the many nights that I sat at the computer well into the early morning hours. She has always provided whatever support was needed, and then some. I would also like to thank my mother for always believing in me, for always supporting me, and for being the best mother anyone could ask for.

Index

Acorn Fund, 36
Actively managed mutual funds, 55
  asset allocation shifts by managers of,
    196–99, 201
  bear market performance, 41
  chasing hot managers, 17, 21, 22–23
  coin-flipping results correlating with
    beating the market, 88–89
  distributions of, 45–49, 179
  emerging market funds, 85–87
  enhanced index funds, 80–84
  fees charged by, 38, 39, 40, 43–44, 81,
    82, 83
  international, 86–87
  investment policy statement and,
    212
  market gurus and, *see* Gurus, market
  newsletter advice on, *see* Newsletters
  operating expenses of, 43, 79, 90, 152,
    231
  past performance as basis of selection,
    17, 19–22
  past performance's predictive value,
    29–30, 52, 225, 229
  Prudent Investor Rule and, 51
  rating of, *see* Ratings of mutual funds
  results of, 1–2, 13, 19–41 *passim*, 62,
    79–80, 87–89, 229–31

  style drift due to, 196–99, 226
  survivorship bias and, 230, 231
  taxes and, 20, 45–49, 179
  trade publication advice on, *see* Trade
    publications
  trading expenses of, 44, 152
  turnover of, 45, 79–80, 87, 95–98
  underperforming a passively managed
    portfolio, 248–50
  underperforming the market, 3, 12–13,
    19–41 *passim*, 59, 73, 79–80,
    85–87, 87–88, 129, 225–26
Active portfolio management, 8–55
  behavioral economics and, 13–14
  belief in, 10
  cocktail party story syndrome and, 16
  efficient markets and, 67–68
  faith in work ethic and, 13
  of fixed income assets, 89–90, 92
  gambler's fallacy and, 15
  love of gambling and, 14–15
  media hype and, 12–13
  operating expenses of, 43, 79, 90,
    152
  reasons for belief in, 12–16
  results of, 5, 10, 84
  small-cap companies and, 84
  timing the market, *see* Market timing

Index

Index

high, risk and returns for companies
with, 126
Booth, David, 86–87, 119
Boston Exchange, 63
Bramwell, Elizabeth, 35
Bramwell, Growth Fund, 35
Brinson, Gary P., 10
Brokerage firms, *see* Investment firms
Bubbles, 78
Buffett, Warren, 42, 75, 98, 226–27
Building a model portfolio, 163–91
    annual checkup, 176, 194
    asset allocation decisions, 163–64
    avoiding too conservative an asset
        class allocation, 182–91
    international equities in, 167–69
    liquidity test, 173–75
    stomach acid test, 169–72
    taxable and non-taxable accounts,
        176–82
    unreasonable expectations and, 172
Bull markets, 75
Business Week:
    Best Buy list of U.S. mutual funds,
        248–50
    "The 100 Best Small Companies,"
        24–25
Buy and hold strategy, 2, 30, 34, 78, 226

Calvert Strategic Growth Fund, 31
Capital gains taxes, 45–49, 51, 178–79
    hold or sell decision and, 245–47
Capital Ideas (Bernstein), 238
Cardano, Girolamo, 15
Carhart, Mark, 79–80, 219, 230
Carlock, Roger, 151
Carpenter Analytical Services, 74
Cars, cash needs for, 173
Cascade Communications, 66
Cash equivalents, 107
Cash needs, liquidity test for, *see*
    Liquidity test
Center for Research in Security Pricing,
    119, 200
Charles Schwab, 47
Chartists, 100
    see also Technical analysis
Chrysler Corporation, 110
Cisco Systems, 66–67

Citicorp, 110–11
Clayton, Michele, 114
Clements, Jonathan, 38, 147–48, 233
CNBC, 18, 33, 254
    technical analysis on, 101, 104
CNN, 252
Coastal Caribbean, 63–64
Cocktail party story syndrome, 16
Coin-flipping results:
    correlating with beating the market,
        88–89
    randomness of markets and, 101–102
Commissions, 2, 77, 151
Competitiveness of investing, 42, 226
Compound growth rate, 138
Compound interest, 215–18
Confidence in your strategy, 6
Confirmations of transactions, 223
Conflicts of interest, 222
Conservative model portfolio, 164
    international equity allocation, 168, 169
Control portfolio, 148–49, 153–54
    changing compositions of, with
        Modern Portfolio Theory, 154–60
Corporate bonds, 105–106, 130–31
    default risk of, 105
Corrections, 34
    fear to flight during, 209
    see also Bear markets; Crashes, stock
        market
Correlation, 139–40
    between bond and equity returns, 123
    diversification and, 140
Cost and efficient markets, 60, 93–99
Craig, James, 35
Crashes, stock market:
    1929, 78
    1987, 72, 78
    forecasting of, 72, 78
    see also Bear markets; Corrections
CREF stock account, 53
Current valuation and efficiency of
    markets, 65–67
Custodian of your assets, 223

Dalbar Financial Services, 219
Data mining, 32
Defensive model portfolio, 164
    international equity allocation, 168–69

287

Index

Index

Index

Inflation:
erosion of purchasing power and, 184–85, 190–91
real rates of return after, 107
risk from, 182–84
Information:
efficient markets theory and, 59–67
insider, 61, 64
rapid spread of, 62–64
Initial public offerings (IPOs), 254–55
"In Search of Excellence: the Investor's Viewpoint," 114
Insider Information, 61, 64
Institutional Investor, 54
Institutional investors, 237
as the market, 42
passive portfolio strategies of, 53–54
research efforts to beat the market, 62
see also Pension funds
Institutional mutual funds, 149–50
Institutional-style mutual funds, 150
Interest, compound, 215–18
Interest rates, forecasting of, 90–92, 121, 129–30
International markets and assets:
allocation between taxable and non-taxable accounts, 179–80
diversification by investing in, 141–43, 154–55, 157–58, 228, 237
efficiency of, 86–87, 118
model portfolio equity allocation to, 167–69
three-factor model and, 126
Internet, spread of information on, 62
Investment advisor, *see* Financial advisors
Investment firms:
advice from, *see* Financial advisors
commissions charged by, *see* Commissions
legend building around expert forecasters, 72–74
Investment objectives, setting, 210–14
Investment pandering, 23–24, 30, 31–32, 226, 253
ignoring of, 6
Investment Policy (Ellis), 238
Investment policy statement, 207–14, 228–29

asset class allocations, 211–12
being in control of, 214
discipline of, 209
establishing period schedule of events and reviews, 213
financial advisor, role of, 214
fixed income allocation, determination of, 209–10
implementing, 214
ladder projecting cash needs, 209
liquidity test for, 209
procedures and controls for monitoring portfolio, 212–13
rebalancing, 212, 213
setting investment objectives, 210–14
stomach acid test for, 209–10
Investment Quality Trends, 32
Investment Strategies for the Twenty-first Century (Armstrong), 238
Investments versus savings, 107–108
IPO myth, 254–55

Janus Fund, 35, 151
Jeffrey, Robert, 49
Job loss, cash needs for, 173
Journal of Finance, 101
Journal of Portfolio Management, 50
Junk bonds, 106, 131

Kahn and Rudd, 37
Kaufman Fund, 35
Kernen, Joe, 33
Keynes, John Maynard, 169
Kiplinger's Personal Finance, 34, 36

Laddered portfolio approach, 185–90, 209, 210, 227
Large-cap asset class, 156–57
allocation between taxable and non-taxable accounts, 179
diversification benefits of, 166
international equities, 165–66
U.S. equities, 165–66
value stocks in, 115
Lee, Dwight, 227
Legend building around expert forecasters, 72–74
Lehman Brothers, 74

Index

Index

Index

Regressing to the mean strategy, 228,
241–44
Rekenthaler, John, 29–30, 198
Research, *see* Information
Retail mutual funds, 151–53
Retired individuals:
  avoiding too conservative an asset
  allocation, 182–84
  laddered portfolio approach for,
  185–90
Returns on investment:
  asset allocation and, 10, 11, 80, 125
  for equities, 107, 187
  five-factor model, 124–33
  market timing and, 10
  with model portfolio, 159–60
  risk and, *see* Risk
  stock picking and, 10
  volatility and, 135–38
  see also specific asset classes
Risk:
  compensation for perceived, 106
  efficient markets theory and, 60,
  105–24
  identifying high-risk asset classes,
  109–11, 227–28
  returns and cost of capital, 106–107
  stomach acid test, *see* Stomach acid
  test
  volatility and, *see* Volatility
  see also specific asset classes
Roberts, Harry, 100–101, 102
Rogers, Jimmy, 252
Rothschild family, 60–61
Russell, Richard, 31
Russell 2000 Index, 24–25

Sales pressure, 12
Samuelson, Paul, 68
Savings, 107
Schwab, Charles, 233
Securities and Exchange Commission
(SEC), 231
SEI Corporation, 19
Seligman Income Fund, 44
Shearson Lehman, 72–73
Shearson Sector Analysis Fund, 73
Shiller, Robert J., 14
Shilling, A. Gary, 91

Shorts, Binkley, 62
Shoven, John, 47
Siegel, Jeremy, 119
Simmons, Kent, 35
Sinquefield, Rex, 38
Small-cap asset class, 161, 228
  active management of, 84
  allocation between taxable and non-
  taxable accounts, 179
  in diversified portfolio, 155–57
  market capitalization of, 200
  risk and return of, 109, 110, 113,
  119–21, 123, 124, 126, 128
  value stocks, 115, 156–57, 228
Smart Money, 18
  Superstar Funds list, 27–28
Smith Barney, 74
Standard & Poor's 500 Index, 37
  active management underperforming,
  3, 12–13, 19–41 *passim,* 59, 73,
  79–80
  growth in investment in, 3
  mutual funds mimicking, 13, 148
  real rate of return, 107
Standard deviation to measure volatility,
136
Statistics and data mining, 32
Statman, Meir, 208
Sterne, Susan, 90–91
Stock, *see* Equities
Stock picking, 10, 237
  basis for, 17
  poor results of, 18–19, 161
Stomach acid test, 169–72, 228
  annual repetition of, 176
  for investment policy statement,
  209–10
Stovall, Robert, 12, 87–88
Stowers, James, III, 35–36
Strong, Richard, 199
Strong Discovery Fund, 198–99
Style drift, 196–201, 205, 226
Summary, 225–33
Superstars, explaining performance of,
98–99
Survivorship bias, 230, 231

Tactical Asset Allocation (TAA), 258–59
Tax-deferred accounts, 47

Index